THE PAST
A...

His...

Alvie and Insh

THE PAST AROUND US

History and the parish of Alvie and Insh

HELEN RUSSELL

DRUMCLUAN BOOKS

ISBN 0-9524965-0-X

Typeset by XL Publishing Services, Nairn
Printed in Great Britain
By Highland News Group, Inverness
For Drumcluan Books
Feshie Bridge, Inverness-shire

CONTENTS

CONTENTS

FOREWORD

This is a light-weight and incomplete account of some of the ways in which history has affected this parish. It began as a very short information sheet about Insh Church; when that was completed there was quite a lot of information in my notes which was 'left over' but seemed too valuable to waste. More research resulted in a collection that was becoming unmanageable... but would never be complete,

This book therefore is an attempt to put the information gathered in some sort of order which it is hoped will entertain and inform, in spite of the many gaps. Other books are mentioned and listed which will extend the reader's knowledge and enjoyment of the past and present - of the history, legends, customs and the people - of this and the surrounding parts of Badenoch.

HELEN RUSSELL, BA Cantab, Dip RE London

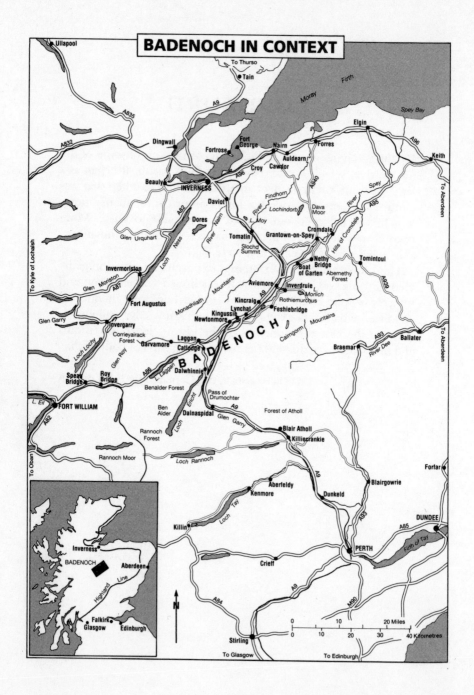

BADENOCH IN CONTEXT

I
THE LOOK OF THE PLACE

It is possible to claim that the parish of Alvie and Insh is in the heart of Scotland – that geographically it lies in the centre of the land-mass of Scotland.

Nowadays the tourist industry claims this area as an excellent centre for touring the whole of Scotland – the sea is only about forty miles away as the crow flies in any direction. The geography of these two parishes, now one parish, has affected (and still does affect) its history, its past, its present and its future.

When you cross Drumochter pass, as you drive up the new A9 from the south, you are entering a world totally different from the rich lands around Perth, the Central Belt, the developed lowlands through which you have been travelling.

The hills rise on either side of the road at the Pass, bleak, and often dark, treeless bare horizons; the grey-black scree with heather which is dark brown at most seasons; bright with young blaeberry leaves in the late spring, orange, yellow, red, with sphagnum moss, sedge grass and bracken in the autumn. In winter the heather looks even darker against the snow; in the early summer the broom and whin make bright banners of yellow along the railway and the river banks.

There are no houses to be seen, no people, no signs of human life along the roadside. (If you are lucky you may in winter see red deer.) As far as the eye can see there are just bare hills – beautiful or stark as the eye of the beholder sees them. This is how you enter Badenoch from the south.

If you come from the north from Inverness over the Slochd pass, the picture is much the same until, leaving the pass, the beauty of the Cairngorm mountain range hits your vision. Bynack, Cairngorm, Ben Macdhui and Braeriach and Carn Ban lie away to the east and south. You are aware, as your eye stretches to their beauty, that you have crossed one barrier of hills and are looking at another one.

From the east, Dava Moor has to be crossed on your way to Badenoch from Nairn; it is a bleak piece of land that I am always very glad not to have to cross on foot; further east the road from Tomintoul is the one most frequently closed by bad weather even today. Then the great hills of the Cairngorm range sweep back to Drumochter. There are ways through these mountains but quite often bad weather makes walking them impossible.

The Monaliadhs to the west of the Spey are gentler hills than the Cairngorms; the Corrieyairack pass, from Fort Augustus in the Great Glen to Laggan on the Spey carries the eighteenth-century road built by General Wade. It is a great feat of engineering which gave Prince Charles Edward a military advantage his opponents had not anticipated; it is not now drivable, but is a right of way, a public road. The only road from the west runs up Glen Spean from the Great Glen, then alongside Loch Laggan and on northward by the Spey to Newtonmore.

So as the maps show, the hills ringing Badenoch are a barrier which has only been easily penetrated since modern roads and vehicles and the railway altered our lives. Even now these passes can be closed by bad weather, Badenoch isolated.

All people living in the Highlands understood the difficulties and perils of travelling, and many songs and prayers for travellers show how ardently spiritual protection was desired, *felt* to be needed. Many of these verses were collected by Alexander Carmichael in his wonderful volumes of 'Carmina Gadelica'.

> Be Thou a smooth way before me.
> Be Thou a guiding star above me.
> Be Thou a keen eye behind me.
> This day, this night, forever.
>
> May God make safe to you each steep,
> May God make open to you each pass,
> May God make clear to you each road,
> And may He take you in the clasp of His own two hands.

God be with you in every pass,
Jesus be with you on every hill,
Spirit be with you on every stream,
Headland and ridge and lawn.
Each sea and land, each moor and meadow
In the trough of the waves, on the crest of the billows,
each step of the journey you go.

You take the point? To reach Badenoch required effort and a pressing need for getting there.

A good place to observe the nature of this land today is at the direction indicator stone at the highest point of the walk-about route of the Highland Wildlife Park that lies to the west of Loch Insh, a mile or so south of Kincraig. There you can see very clearly the strath, the surrounding hills, and the nature of both, but it must be remembered that what we see today is modified by thousands of years of man's attempts to make the land support him.

You will see, southwards, between Loch Insh and Kingussie, the Insh Marshes; 'Badenoch' means 'drowned land' and indeed these marshes are frequently flooded, so much so that the course of the river Spey can sometimes only be traced by the line of bushy, stunted-looking trees growing on top of the built-up banks. The rest of the very low land, further south by Newtonmore and Laggan, floods much less than in former times because of man's efforts to drain it and to build flood banks, altering the look of the landscape.

Northwards from Loch Insh, the river Feshie coming often in spate from the hills, brings boulders and gravel down to raise a blockage at its junction with the Spey, causing more flooding. Men have built a causeway from the east side of the strath, at the foot of Loch Insh and now it is linked to the west side by a bridge. Formerly the causeway reached only to the church on Tom Eunan and one crossed the Spey by a ferry – the Boat of Insh. The shinty pitch to the north of the road on the causeway was once part of Loch Insh, and is again under water as I write.

Looking around you from this vantage point you will see that the upper slopes of the hills are 'moorland' – heather, sedge grasses, blaeberry, cowberry, bear berry… mosses of many kinds, ground willow, with lichen-covered rocks, both large and small, shaping the hills. Man, and his domestic animals, has de-forested much of the land below the natural treeline, which is approximately 2000 feet above sea-level. The bulldozed ground on either side of the new A9 reveals the sandy and stony nature of the soil.

You will see how modern forestry has covered large areas with 'blanket' forestry plantations – spruces, pines, some larch – particularly noticeable in the lower Glen Feshie area. The lower slopes of the strath are more likely to be pasture than plough; sheep are predominant, cattle more scarce, though there are more nowadays than there used to be. There is also a deer farm at Rothiemurchus.

Birch, aspens, rowan and geans (wild cherry) flower magnificently in spring, and colour dramatically in autumn; there are many oaks, though fewer than in the past, some ash, willows of different kinds, and of course the pines; beech grows well and the trees, together with the heather and bracken make this area beautiful past belief at all seasons; but it is a hard land in which to live, and often enough, a hard land through which to travel.

2

TRAVELLERS

The first people to come to Badenoch were not really travellers but people moving in from the coastal areas to make new settlements in a place which would be able to support them. They probably arrived here by moving up the banks of the Spey which would have been the easiest route. This wide glacier-formed strath, with Glenmore extending it, allowed conditions in which continuously used settlements could be developed, though these earliest settlements would have left few traces.

Parts of Rothiemurchus and further north, some parts of Abernethy Forest, still retain areas where the ground has not been disturbed by man since the Ice Age, though tree-felling has taken place. There, and on islands where there has been no grazing, such as the islands of Loch Laggan, is visible the kind of vegetation and the conditions through which would-be travellers had to make their way.

The difficult terrain – thick woods, crags, steep and rocky hills, marsh and loch – all limited human activity, especially in earlier centuries before tools were developed. Badenoch may be central to the land mass of Scotland, but this meant that 'history' happened in areas easier of access. Tracks and roads developed only slowly.

The existence of ancient stone circles shows that settlers were moving in this strath in Neolithic times. Later, Druidic priests and tribal leaders probably came here; Christian missionaries certainly did. Later still as the kingdom of Scotland became more organised, and the church too, there was more contact between Badenoch and the outside world of earls and bishops and clan leaders – and the Law.

By the seventeenth century Badenoch did become involved in more of the national events, mostly as a pathway for warring forces. The conflicts of King and Parliament, of the Covenanters and King, the Jacobite-Hanoverian struggles – brought Montrose across the hills to Badenoch; later his kinsman, Viscount Dundee, raising the clans for James VII, used this area for some of his winning manoeuvres. Jacobite efforts brought troubles thereafter, with march and counter march through Badenoch. (I will write of all this more fully later.)

Then came the roads. Letters written in the early 1700s reveal the urgent need for roads; the 'pacification of the Highlands' required them. The novel *The New Road* by Neil Munro shows clearly and painfully the need – and the effects of – the development of a road system in the Highlands.

We are given marvellous insight into the nature of life in the Highlands, and in and around Inverness, by a series of letters sent in the years following 1726 by a government surveyor, Captain Burt, to a friend in London. Burt also travelled down the Great Glen, and even through Badenoch to Blair Atholl and Edinburgh. He did not like most of what he saw!

'I shall conclude this Description of the outward appearance of the mountain… a disagreeable Subject… not much variety in it, but gloomy spaces, different rocks, heaths high and low, … and the whole of a dismal gloomy Brown drawing upon a dirty Purple; and most disagreeable of all when the Heath is in Bloom.'

'But of all the views, I think the most horrid is to look at the Hills from East to West, or vice versa, for then the eye penetrates far among them and sees more particularly their stupendous Bulk, frightful irregularity and horrid gloom.' (Perhaps I should add that Burt's idea of a beautiful view was Richmond Park, in south-west London.)

That roads were needed is amply supported by Burt's description of his travels; 'the old Ways (for Roads I will not call them) consisted chiefly of stony Moors. Bogs, rugged, rapid Fords, Declivities of Hill, entangling Woods and giddy Precipices.' There are descriptions of overcoming hill 'Ways' that are 'almost impractical for a horse with his rider,' and likewise 'a rocky Way where we were obliged to dismount, and sometimes to climb and otherwhile to slide down. But what vexed me most of all, they called it a Road.' Fords were very dangerous and bridges non-existent. At the end of Burt's letters there is fine description of how he planned to build the roads and bridges.

Another system of trackways developed in the eighteenth and early nineteenth centuries – the 'drove roads'. These were developed from earlier routes but grew to a well-recognised and much used system. The droving traffic was the outcome of increasing markets for beef in the south and the increased cattle breeding activities in the north, developed to meet the demand. Cattle were the only form of readily available wealth which – though with considerable exertion – was transportable. It has been said that the cattle droving trade was the beginning of the capitalist system in the Highlands and led to the end of the Highland system of farming and trade. A study of the whole process of droving yields an enormous amount of information, both about the lifestyles of the country through which the droves passed, and about the farming systems.

As far as Badenoch was concerned there were no really big gathering centres, though some of the Moray beasts gathered in fair quantities on the Nethy, just north of Ryvoan bothy, on land cleared of the old Abernethy Forest. One route which crossed Badenoch came down over the Slochd pass from Inverness by Aviemore, Kincraig and Pitmain, to cross the Drumochter pass at Dalwhinnie. Some herds might break off at Aviemore to go by the Larig Ghru and Glenfernate to Kirkmichael and then by Balinluig, or Amulree, to Crieff. At Kincraig some herds took off up Glen Feshie to join these routes. Another route came over the Corrieyairack and by Garvamore to join the Drumochter Pass route, past Cat Lodge; this would have included beasts from Skye as well as from the whole north-west of Scotland.

These routes, together with the 'Government' roads, resulted in Badenoch becoming more integrated into the kingdom of Scotland. The later coachroad brought government officers to enforce the authority of the central government, replacing the clan jurisdiction which was destroyed by acts of Parliament after the '45.

By 1838 – a hundred years after Captain Burt had made his

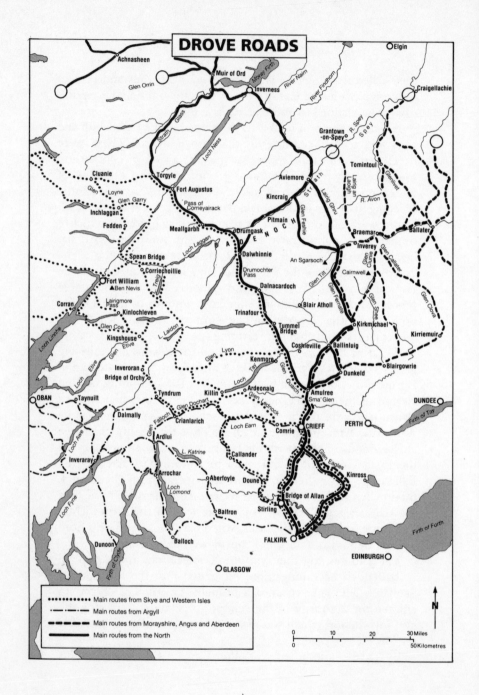

DROVE ROADS

○ Elgin

Achnasheen

Muir of Ord

Glen Orrin

○ Craigellachie

Inverness

River Nairn

River Findhorn

R. Spey

Grantown -on-Spey

Spey

Tomintoul

Glenlivet

Strath Glass

Loch Ness

Cluanie

Torgyle

Aviemore

R. Avon

Glen

Loyne

Fort Augustus

Kincraig

Laing an Laggan

Glen Garry

Pass of Corrieyairack

Pitmain

Laing Ghru

Braemar○

Ballater○

Inchlaggan

Fedden○

Meallgarbh

Drumgask

Strath

Inverey○

Fort Augustus

BADENOCH

Dalwhinnie

An Sgarsoch ▲

Glen Clunie

Glen Callater

Loch Laggan

Spean Bridge

Drumochter Pass

Cairnwell ▲

Glen Tilt

Corriechoillie

Dalnacardoch

Glen Feardar

Treig

Fort William
▲Ben Nevis

Blair Atholl

Kirkmichael

Glen Shee

Glen Clova

Corran

Lairigmore Pass

Trinafour

Glen Fernate

Kirriemuir

Loch Linnhe

Kinlochleven

Tummel Bridge

Loch Etive

Glen Coe

L. Laidon

Coshieville

Ballinluig

Kingshouse

Glen Lyon

Kenmore

Glen Quaich

Dunkeld

Blairgowrie

Inveroran

Glen Etive

Loch Tay

Bridge of Orchy

Ardeonaig

Amulree

OBAN○

Taynuilt

Tyndrum

Killin

Glen Lednock

Sma' Glen

DUNDEE○

Dalmally

Loch Awe

Glen Falloch

Glen Dochart

Crianlarich

Loch Earn

Comrie

CRIEFF

PERTH○

Firth of Tay

Ardlui

L. Katrine

Callander

Doune

Glen Eagles

Kinross

Inveraray○

Arrochar

Aberfoyle

Loch Fyne

Loch Lomond

Balfron

Bridge of Allan

Stirling

Firth of Forth

Dunoon

Balloch

FALKIRK○

Firth of Clyde

EDINBURGH○

○GLASGOW

N

●●●●●●●●● Main routes from Skye and Western Isles

─·─·─·─ Main routes from Argyll

─ ─ ─ ─ Main routes from Morayshire, Angus and Aberdeen

─────── Main routes from the North

0   10   20   30 Miles
0   50 Kilometres

first survey of the 'Roads of the Highlands' – Lord Cockburn, the famous Edinburgh judge, was making his 'Circuit Journeys', and has left a journal with revealing comments on the land and the people. Looking at the 'village dwellings' in Lochaber – and no doubt they were similar to the ones in Badenoch – he has written 'The difference between these quiet little Indian wigwam-looking hamlets when seen at a distance and their utter abomination when approached... it is horrid that human life should be passed in these disgusting holes.' (I would think they were vastly preferable to some of the 'holes' to be found in Edinburgh.)

Apart from the inference that by this date the system of Law worked in the Highlands (the cynical message passed by one member of a family to another was 'Look after yourself; the Law has reached Ross-shire!'), the speeds of Lord Cockburn's travel must be noted. In April 1838 he left Kindrogan (about 10 miles south of Blair Atholl) at 11.00 am... and arrived at Aviemore by 3.00 pm – 65 miles in four hours, by coach, indicates a very good road. In April 1839 travelling south from Aviemore to Dunkeld he wrote 'We have seen only two gigs, the mail coach, and under a dozen carts. The snow was thick in some places, and Loch Garry totally frozen over.' In 1842, passing Glen Truim ('a strange wild place') he slept at the Gordon Arms Hotel and not at the private dwelling of Pitmain Lodge, as he had done previously. Lord Cockburn's views of landscape may appear as strange to us as Burt's; he writes of the 'wretched larch' which disfigures the landscape and says that Aviemore 'would be the grandest inland place, had it a castle and a wood', he commends the woods of oak and chestnut opposite the Doune, but 'it is necessary to get rid of the "abominable Larch"'.

When Queen Victoria came north in 1842, staying first at Ardverikie, the 'romantic' view of the Highlands began to come into fashion. Ardverikie proved too wet for her, and she settled in Deeside. The Queen's descriptions of the Cairngorms show her keen delight in the 'scenery', and her warm accounts of the people she met show her deep appreciation of the people who lived here. It is a totally different picture from that given by

Captain Burt a hundred years earlier, yet one can recognise the same features in both landscape and people. (See Note 1, Queen Victoria's Highland Expeditions, p89.)

By the late 1860s came the railways, gradually bringing an amazing change to the towns and villages of Badenoch. The centres of population changed to locate themselves round the new stations. This can be seen by the position of the local schools; following the Education Act of 1872 schools were built nationwide, and here they were naturally built in what were thought to be sites central to the population. But now at Alvie, Aviemore, Boat of Garten and Duthill, the schools are all some distance from where most of the children live nowadays; some new schools have been built and are an indicator of the size and the centres of our population today.

The first railway guides reveal a picture substantially different from that put out by the tourist office today. (See Note 2, Guide Books, p90.) The railways brought the 'summer visitors' whose presence in this area altered it in many ways. Many stone villas were built in this period which altered the style of the villages and towns. Many folk from other parts of Scotland came here to work on the railways, and houses were built for them also. Some of the visitors built houses and settled here. Meta Scarlett in her book of reminiscences *In the Glens where I was Young* gives a vivid picture of the way life was affected by these changes, and the interaction between old and new features of daily living. (See Note 3, The Railways, p91.)

The first car-borne tourists came to explore and enjoy the countryside and to stay for quite a while. Nowadays, tourists can come for the day only – a day's fishing, shooting, skiing, climbing or walking – and be away again to the Central Belt by nightfall. Between these two extremes – the visitors who came for three months and those who come for the day – there has been every kind of visitor, some of whom have become 'settlers' themselves. With them have come those who serve their needs. We have New Zealand ski-instructors, Canadian hotel workers, people from all parts of Britain and the world. Thus the population of this parish is a mixture without old class divisions though the estates of Balavil, Dunachton, Alvie, and Kinrara and Rothiemurchus are still the main landowners, together with the Forestry Commission and the RSPB.

It is the 'travellers' – tourists – who provide most incomes in the parish now. Perhaps the modern systems of communications may result in 'second-homers' becoming real settlers, permanent residents, and a new chapter developing for the parish of Alvie and Insh.

3
HISTORY

Pre-history or 'it may well have been...'

History is the story of the past for which there is evidence. Legends embroider history, and myths add colour and shape often with poetic imagination. In trying to recount the story of the past here in this parish much slips into the category of 'it may well have been that...'. Traditional stories must not be disregarded but for all that they are not, by themselves, 'history'.

We can think of the story of the events which occurred here under two main headings; the ways in which outside forces influenced people's lives (and that can also be divided into the effects of central government and the effects of religion and church government) and secondly, the ways in which the people living here altered their own lives and the lives of their neighbours.

As I have suggested, the earliest dwellers in the area, Neolithic man, probably came up the Spey to found new settlements in an area which would be able to support them. The glacier-formed strath of the upper Spey does allow conditions in which farming – settled, not nomadic farming – could be developed. The earliest settlements would have left few traces, but later the people built stone circles which seem similar to the Clava Cairns beside the River Nairn near Cawdor. These Clava Cairns have been excavated and much information obtained from them, and many other circles thought to be of the same type have been located. (See Note 4, The Clava Cairns, p93.)

Within our area, we have visible the stone circles at Aviemore and Easter Delfour which have been charted but not excavated. 'It may well have been' that the customs, lifestyles and beliefs of the folk who built them were similar to those people living close to the Moray Firth. Excavation here would enlighten us much more, and perhaps enable us to estimate the size of the population. That there was movement between the Moray coast and Badenoch is shown by the evidence of these circles. It is sad there is not more to look at by Delfour, and the Aviemore circle is oppressed by the houses built so closely around it.

Nonetheless, there they are – witness to a people who had strong ideas of what should be done in matters of worship and of thought for the dead.

These people thought these matters were so important that they took the immense pains necessary to build these circles and set up the standing stones. We may not understand the true import of this labour but we are taught something about these people just by looking at their remaining works.

During the first or second century AD or even earlier, the souterrain on the hill above the new A9 just south of Lynchat was built. It was probably designed for emergency storage and as an emergency hide-out. It is magnificently built – the bit of it you can see; again it is from excavations elsewhere that the function of this horse-shoe shaped massive shelter/store is assumed. Its existence shows that raiders were expected, though there is no knowing who they were or whence they came. The inhabitants of the now vanished medieval castle of Raitts probably used it.

Above the souterrain on the hillside are the mounds of a seventeenth-century village, occupied until the nineteenth century. Higher still, on what is now moorland, are the round humps of early houses, similar to the remains of Pictish houses; it could be that they are grain stores, though there are rather too many of them. A little to the north and higher on the hillside, there are remains of old walls and ditches that seem defensive rather than agricultural. There is a vitrified hill-fort above Dunachton.

The course of events in Central Scotland in very early times – say, up to 800 AD – is difficult to establish clearly. Early chroniclers do not agree on dates, names are written with many variations, and many characters bore the same name. Furthermore, most chronicles were written to establish a particular view of history, to underline the greatness and power of certain leaders. Legends and even myths find their way into many 'histories'.

Also access to Badenoch was difficult, as has been pointed out, so that the major events which shaped our history were fought out or happened elsewhere. The impact of national events on Badenoch is hard to assess.

By the time history came to be written about these parts, Scotland was almost wholly peopled by those tribes which came to be known as 'Picts'. These were probably the descendants of the indigenous iron-age tribes of Indo-European origin. The name 'Picts' (taken from a Latin poem of 297 AD) is probably a nickname meaning 'the painted ones', but though we have no real name for the whole race, we do have names for different tribes.

The people living in Badenoch belonged to the Pictish tribe *Caledonii* (this is the origin of the name sometimes applied to all the Highlands – *Caledonia*). We still talk of the ancient woodlands of Abernethy and Rothiemurchus as being 'remnants of Caledonian forests'. The Picts left no writings, except the King Lists, from which much can be learnt, but we have inherited a wonderful legacy of carved stones, pillars, slabs, crosses – the 'Pictish Symbol Stones.'

The earliest carvings were simple line-drawings of a fascinating style, incised on hard-wearing stone. Later the carvings were made in relief as well, and many – perhaps most – stones had a collection of several symbols on them. Finally, there were Christian symbols as well. Some of the stones recorded battles, conquests, some had hunting scenes; but most have beautiful if inexplicable, designs on them, some of which may be genealogical, perhaps displaying the heraldic quarterings of the tribal leader and his family, and perhaps the land which he controlled. They are certainly a wonderful heritage, speaking of a highly organised and artistic people.

In this parish only one Pictish symbol stone has been found. It is at Dunachton; it is a slab of diorite stone approximately 4 feet long, by 16 inches wide, and 4½ inches thick. A deer's head is incised on it – just the one symbol – but it shows grace and definition of great artistry. (See Note 5, The Pictish Symbol Stone, p94.) The head is similar in style and design to one at

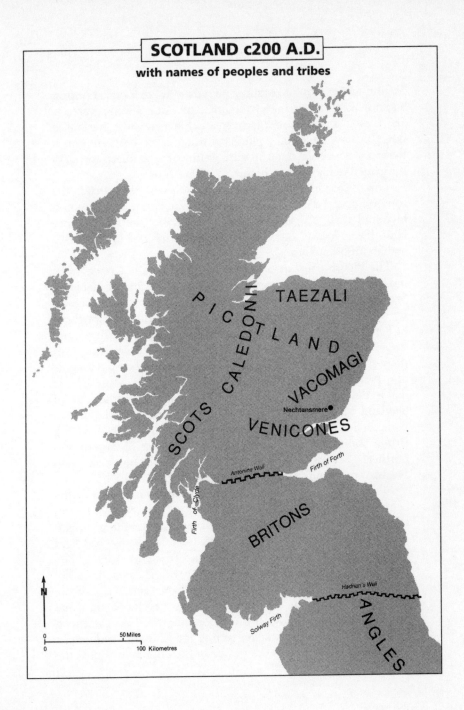

SCOTLAND c200 A.D.
with names of peoples and tribes

TAEZALI

PICTLAND

SCOTS CALEDONII

VACOMAGI

Nechtansmere ●

VENICONES

Antonine Wall

Firth of Forth

Firth of Clyde

BRITONS

Hadrian's Wall

Solway Firth

ANGLES

N

| 0 | 50 Miles |
| 0 | 100 Kilometres |

Strathmiglo in Fife, and to those carved on stones found at Ardross and now kept in Inverness Museum. The stone was discovered in 1870, used as a lintel in a farm steading which was being pulled down. It now stands on a plinth on which it has been erected, at the top of a wooded slope 50 yards south of the southern corner of the garden of Dunachton Lodge. (35 NH 820046).

This beautiful carving, the few stones of the circles, the souterrain, and the mounds covering unknown, undated houses, forts and walls, are all we have as evidence of the early history here. (See Note 6, Sites of archeological interest in Badenoch and Strathspey, p95.)

The Pictish tribal organisation has left only a few traces here, but one of them is the name Dunachton, the fort of Nechtan. Standing above the north-west end of Loch Insh is Dunachton Lodge, thought to be built on the site of the Pictish stronghold of King Nechtan. This idea is reinforced by the Pictish symbol stone, already described, found there. In the Pictish King Lists there are three King Nechtans, the first and third being outstanding. Nechtan, son of the powerful King Brude, achieved the major defeat of the Angles at Nechtansmere in the east of Scotland in 685. The King Nechtan whose fort dominated Badenoch was probably the son of Derelei, who succeeded King Brude about 720 and ruled over a wide area of eastern and northern Scotland. Bede, the early English historian, calls Nechtan the 'king of the Picts of North Britain'.

Nechtan died in 732 and during the following years of the century there was considerable fighting between the Pictish tribes, the incoming Scots of Dalriada and the invading Angles. The legendary Arthurian campaigns (c450 onwards) had kept back the Saxons both in the north and south of Britain. The main areas of warfare were, however, outwith Badenoch. In 852 Kenneth MacAlpine, King of Scots, became also King of the Picts, and from then on Scotland slowly developed into one united kingdom. As the organisation improved so Badenoch gradually became more integrated into the Kingdom and we can note the development of the power of the church as well as the power of the Crown.

4

THE INFLUENCE OF THE CHURCH

The Pictish tribes who came to rule the whole of Scotland long after the makers of the stone circles had vanished, probably followed a druidical religion. (See Note 7, Druids, p96.) In the years following the establishment of St. Ninian's Christian Church at Whithorn in 397 AD Christian missionaries penetrated much of mainland Scotland. There had been Christians in Britain under the Roman rule, but that faded from Scotland before 400 AD. It was the early Church, the teams of Christian missionaries, who first touched the inhabitants of Badenoch with any thought of belonging to a greater community than that of the immediately neighbouring tribes. Cell by cell the missionary monks, first from Ninian's foundation at Whithorn, then from Columba's Iona monastery and training centre, established some knowledge of Christ's kingdom.

From Whithorn – where Ninian had made his base at 'The White House' or 'Candida Casa' – Ninian's monks did penetrate very many areas of Scotland, with varying degrees of success. The tradition remains, endorsed by Professor Douglas Simpson, that Saint Moluag, an Irish Pict, who died at Ardclach in about 500 AD, came from Lismore by the Great Glen to Fort Augustus and by Inverfarigaig to Lynchat. There he established a cell, a Christian teaching base. The area is still known as Chapel Park, and this is probably where the Gospel was first preached in Badenoch.

The pattern of mission work was to build a cell for the monk and his companions in an area which had a clear grassy space around it, which could be used for the gathering of the people, who would be summoned to a time of Gospel preaching by the ringing of a hand-bell, such as the one still hanging in Insh Church.

It seems that some cells failed to continue as Christian bases, and the lack of follow-up left Christian teaching undeveloped, indeed often falling back into superstition and paganism. By 563, when Columba began his missionary journeys from Iona, he often found he had to 're-convert' areas where St Donan and others had been. This is not strange, considering the scarcity of copies of any parts of the Scriptures, the almost total illiteracy of the population, and so few to teach others by precept, example or rote. However, it must not be forgotten that the bardic tradition, so very strong, using oral tradition, folk memory and music, was a tool that could also be used for carrying the Gospels.

During his fifty years on Iona, Columba established many Christian cells and probably renewed some of those established earlier. Columba himself reached Inverness and converted the surrounding area (then ruled by the strong king, Brude). It must remain doubtful if Columba himself ever reached Badenoch, though some historians have identified Loch Insh as the scene of one of Columba's major visions – this possibility cannot be ruled out. Tradition is strong that Christianity was established very early on Tom Eunan, the hillock at the north end of Loch Insh where Insh Church stands. It is possible that if the Iona monks worked eastwards from Inverness along the Moray coast – and there are early Christian settlements in support of this... if they reached the Dee (this is now pure supposition), the easiest way back to Iona would be up the Dee, up the Geldie westwards, down the Feshie, pausing at the north end of Loch Insh where there was an ancient ferry... establishing a Christian cell there... and so back by Loch Laggan to the Great Glen, and so by the sea lochs to Iona... People living here are very aware of this route to the west. They could also (as later travellers did) come up Glen Spean and along Loch Laggan; there is above Loch Laggan another early Christian foundation linked by tradition to St Kenneth, a friend and relative of Columba's. However there is also a school of thought that the linking of these churches with these saints is medieval.

In 1900 the Rev William Forsyth, minister of Abernethy and

Kincardine, wrote in his book *Under the shadow of Cairngorm*, that St Kenneth, 'a trusted companion of St. Columba', was 'responsible for the hold of Iona on the area.' He continues 'It was extremely probable that Columba in the course of his labours paid repeated visits to the valley of the Spey, actually founding a church at Kingussie.' Forsyth lists chapels at Laggan (Kenneth's), Kingussie (Columba's), Banchor, (Bridget's), Insh (St Eunan's), and St Drostan's, below Dunachton – all attesting to the power of the Columban church in upper Strathspey. There was certainly a May-time Columban Fair taking place in Kingussie as late as 1886.

If there was a Columban foundation, a Christian cell, on Loch Insh, it is certainly probable that St Adamnan, a later Abbot of Iona, and St Columba's biographer, (who died in 704), might have visited it, as he did most of the other Columban cells. The tradition is very strong that the bronze hand-bell hanging in Insh Church is 'Adamnan's Bell'. It is one of only five bronze hand-made bells remaining in Scotland. Dr Cormac Bourke, an expert on hand-bells, has examined the bell and thinks that on strong typological evidence the bell was probably made around 900, by a travelling craftsman. I like to think it could have been made at Baldow, the local forge.

As Adamnan died in 704, this is unsatisfactory to those of us who would like to think of it as Adamnan's bell. Certainly we can believe that it was made for the Christian centre on Tom Eunan, at the north end of Loch Insh, and is some evidence for long-continued worship here. During medieval times, the bell, like many other revered objects, was credited with the gift of healing – and with the powers of speech and flight! The story goes that having been stolen from the church and taken towards Dunkeld, it flew back over the Pass of Drumochter crying 'Tom Eunan! Tom Eunan!' until it reached its home in the church here. The bell is held in affection as our link with the prayers and the preaching of the Gospel of past centuries, a reminder of God's faithfulness to man.

Adamnan, Abbot of Iona from 685 to 704, the outstanding churchman of his day, was in touch with Nechtan, King of the northern Picts, over a long period. Apart from the power struggles among the Picts, and between the Picts and the Scots of Dalriada, there was also a serious division because the Christian Picts of north Britain, including those who lived in Badenoch, followed the old Celtic patterns of Church organisation and not the 'Roman' style. The dating of Easter, the rituals of baptism and the rules of monastic foundations were the main points of difference which had arisen from a long period of separation and lack of communication which had allowed each Church to develop differently. This was due to the chaos during the slow break-up of the Roman Empire and the anarchy that followed. Adamnan, perhaps surprisingly, sided with the Roman position and was influential in establishing it in Britain, He had set up a small teaching monastery at Dull in Perthshire, on the upper Tay. Nechtan spent several periods there and his acceptance of the Roman rulings was no doubt derived from Adamnan's teachings. Nechtan even abandoned his kingdom and spent ten years at Dull, then returned and attempted to win his kingdom back. This must have been troublesome for his people here!

At first the control of Christian mission stations was based on the monasteries, to which monks working in these outlying mission cells owed obedience. Thus in the 7th, 8th, and 9th centuries Badenoch looked to Iona for leadership. When Iona was sacked by the Vikings, for some time the Christians in Badenoch looked to Dunkeld for help. The ordination of priests had always rested with the Bishops, and this led in time to the organisation of a system of dioceses and parishes and a lessening of the power of the monasteries.

In the period before the Church became nationally organised, there lived in remote areas, sometimes in groups though not in monasteries under the control of an abbot, holy men who gave themselves up to prayer and meditation and who were often involved in teaching the local population. The name given to this class of holy people is 'Culdees' or 'Ceilide' or Churchmen. They used hand-bells such as the bell found in Insh Church to summon people to a teaching session or to worship. There exists a letter from the organisers of the 'History Exhibition' in

Glasgow in 1911 asking the Session of the parish of Insh for the loan of 'the Culdee bell', which indicates how the bell was regarded at that time. The earliest buildings on Tom Eunan were probably the round cells of the monks, later the dwellings of the 'Culdees'. As no excavation has been done, there is no way of being certain. Tradition names the place for St Adamnan (Eunan is a diminutive of Adamnan), but it is not known when this tradition began. As has been seen, scholars do not always agree.

Elsewhere the influence of the Culdees was superseded by that of the Benedictine monasteries which became centres of learning and Christian faith throughout Europe. Since no monastery was established here the people of Badenoch were left without that enlightenment.

Thus this part of Badenoch was linked with the main strands of history by the early stone circles and their settlements, the Pictish symbol stone betokening the Pictish tribal organisation, and the bronze hand-bell of early Christian missions and the Iona tradition.

Our knowledge of early Christian Scotland is really very scanty, and though Queen Margaret – Saint Margaret, wife of Malcolm Canmore (1057-93) – did tremendous work in increasing true knowledge of the Gospels, we cannot tell whether her efforts reached any in Badenoch. The earliest written mention of Insh Church is in 1190 when it was listed as a parish church. Parishes were formed where churches already existed, so we can presume a church here before that date. The system of parishes and dioceses only slowly developed, and there was often little real control. (At one time Insh was listed as belonging to the diocese of Caithness.) Insh Church and parish are listed again in 1203, and again, along with Kingussie, in 1226. In 1229 the parish was 'erected with all its fruits' into a prebend of Elgin Cathedral by Andrew, Bishop of Moray, and is recorded as paying its dues in 1229, 1289, 1303, 1366, 1467, 1539. (One wonders about the other years – were no dues paid, no dues recorded or were the records lost?)

Alvie Church has a similar history, though probably beginning later. Alvie, known also in some records as Skeiralloway, was dedicated either to St Ailbhe, 'a saint of the Culdees', or to St Drostan, who was a sixth-century abbot of Deer in Buchan, and a relative of St Columba. The small ruined chapel below Dunachton is also dedicated to St Drostan.

Alvie was granted a church by Thomas Randolph, Earl of Moray, in 1331, and its dues were to support the chaplaincies of Moray Cathedral, with whom the patronage remained. The grant was for 'a vicarage perpetual'.

There is a plaque in Alvie Church recording the ministers of Alvie from 1567 to the present day, (See Note 8, List of Ministers, p98) which gives us a sense of continuity. The records of the parish of Alvie are also scarce; in 1713 it was written that Thomas Macpherson, the pastor of Alvie from 1662 to 1708, lost all the records 'in a fire at Invereshie'.

The spellings of Alvie vary greatly, with its translation from Gaelic, Ailbhe, 'island of swans' in 1350, Alveth, later, Alwetht, Alway; in 1400, Alvecht, in 1603, Alwvey, later Alloway, Alvah or Alva.

Tithes from the Badenoch parishes went mainly to Elgin, though Rothiemurchus, Duthill and Kincardine were in 1224 temporarily annexed to the Chapel Royal at Stirling. Kingussie is listed alongside Alvie and Insh without any indication at all of which parish might be richer or larger; the population and wealth of each were probably similar. It is necessary to remember that right into this century dues were paid in kind; at first almost entirely in cattle, sometimes with meal; cheese and butter formed part of the payments at times, as well as wedders (wether lambs). In 1674 'threescore and nineteen wedders ' were sent from the whole area.

In 1597, a James Melville was visiting the Highlands with a number of Commissioners from the General Assembly of the Church of Scotland (then in its infancy) and recounts that 'Badenoch is wild and almost inaccessible' but that the inhabitants were admirable folk though their manner of life was deplorable with almost total ignorance and great poverty; but he writes 'I am sure gif Christ were pretched among them they would schame many lawland professours.' The churches at Alvie and Insh, it seems, had not been able to preach Christ to many with sufficient power.

During and immediately after the Reformation it is probable that parishes were quite often without ministers. The Rev William Forsyth, minister of Abernethy and Kincardine, writes that in 1658 the people ('Heritors and wadsetters', ie the lairds and the better off), 'being unite', and the same folk of Rothiemurchus and Glenmore 'being unite', all petitioned that the money saved by stipends not being paid during vacancies – might be used to set up schools. (It was money to the tune of about 500 merks, a sizeable sum from a 3-year and a 5-year vacancy.) They did not succeed, and grumbles about the lack of schools continued.

The Reformation in Badenoch was apparently not an aggressive movement. In Kingussie a wooden partition was put up in the old Priory Church, and those who held to the old ways worshipped in the chancel, while the followers of the Reformed Church worshipped in the nave on the other side of the partition.

This was, of course, a Gaelic-speaking area; as late as 1894 Insh was listed as one of the many parishes where it was necessary for the minister to speak Gaelic; children were still joining the school in Kingussie in the 1920s with no English.

The Bible was not published in Gaelic until 1783, although translations had been made though not published, from 1680 onwards. This slowed the Reformation in the Highlands, though the Psalms appeared in a Gaelic metrical version around 1660, and the Gaelic Shorter Catechism was available after 1650.

The Reformation did reduce the prayers known by heart (especially the Latin ones) and also the old Gaelic hymns and songs. Liturgy was discarded by the Reformed Church, though this had not been John Knox's wish. The oral memory of the Western Highlands has preserved for us some of the hymns and prayers that would have been common in these parts also till the late nineteenth century. These reveal the traditions of prayer and religious thought taught by the earliest Celtic Christian missionaries and surviving until today; it is a marvellous inheritance.

The most famous of these Celtic prayers may be St. Patrick's Breastplate, but many more remain. Dr Alexander Carmichael faithfully and brilliantly collected many in his wonderful volumes 'Carmina Gaedelica'; these prayers are very much part of everyday living and working, reflecting the Gaelic theology that God is in all His creation, in every part of life, not just in the 'spiritual'. There are prayers for smooring the fire, fetching the cows home, for all common tasks of the day; for travel, seafaring, for new homes, for births, marriages and deaths. These two examples will illustrate their power and depth.

A prayer for protection

As Thou wast before me at my life's beginning
Be Thou so again at my journey's end.
As Thou wast beside me at my soul's shaping,
Father, be Thou also at my journey's end.

****

Thou, my soul's healer, keep me at even, keep me at morning;
Keep me at noon, on rough course faring.
Help and safeguard my means this night,
I am tired, astray and stumbling, shield me from sin.

Thomas Sinton, minister of Dores around 1900, collected both prayers and songs of all sorts from this area and from around Laggan. The collection – entitled 'The Poetry of Badenoch' – is divided into 'Songs of Feeling' 'Songs of War' 'Songs of the Chase' 'Songs of the Soul' and other sections dealing with its people, legends and local events, and it reveals a marvellous amount of humour in the stories and songs showing the values and attitudes among our predecessors here. Today we lack the ceilidhs and gatherings at which these were shared, and we have no outlet for thoughts and feelings. (The local newspaper is a poor substitute.)

The historian James Kirk writes that church affairs in the early seventeenth century are 'shrouded in mystery'. It is true that we cannot tell whether the chief effect of the Reformation was to remove all the support the church had given in rural areas such as this, leaving people to their own devices, or whether the thinking of the Reformation stimulated people to form their own image of the Christian faith though here illiteracy must have limited true Christian growth.

Lowland areas, where the Reformed Church grew best and are best recorded, cannot be taken as examples of what happened in the Highlands. Certainly the Roman Catholic Church did its best to maintain the old links.

Before the Reformation about half the population of Scotland lived north of the Tay, but the number of parishes in this huge land mass was only a fifth of the total number of the parishes of Scotland. Thus parishes here were overlarge, unwieldy, and often most strangely linked, and thus very difficult to serve.

Huntly, the ruling Chief, was himself a Roman Catholic, but did actually appoint Protestant ministers to benefices in his patronage. In 1625 he restored the church at Kingussie, as well as appointing a Protestant minister. Better finances were arranged for the kirk after 1573 (early years for the Church of Scotland); some stipends, including those of Insh, and Alvie, were only £8 or £14 per annum, but Laggan, Abernethy, Advie and Cromdale are listed as £26, while Elgin is given as £56 the same year. In this Presbytery, Inveravon was considered a danger to the Reformed Kirk, since it maintained its Roman Catholic training centre, and Badenoch was reputed to draw 'all quhom they might conquise to their pernicious wayes of both men and women.' In 1627 the Minister at Kingussie was instructed to notify the date of the next celebration of communion 'unto his whole people bot specialle to gang to such as he suspects most within his bounds, taking with him 2 or 3 witnesses to desyr them to communicate – so nain pretend ignorance.' We may presume there was something of the same uncertainty about the religious allegiance of the folk of these parishes too.

In 1626 the parishes of Alvie and Laggan were, albeit unsuitably, linked. Laggan had an incapacitated minister 'of verie great age, infirme in body and hes no thing of the Irish language, quhilk be thair vulgar,' and he himself 'earnestly craved to be disburdened of that charge quhairn he found himselff able to do no guid.' In belated recognition that 'no man in any measure can be able to serve baith parishes' the old minister was finally retired. Later, two qualified recruits capable of restoring the Gospel in Badenoch 'quhilk lyeth destitut of the comfort of the word and sacraments, for the most part altogeidder without disciplin quhairby the gretest part (of Badenoch) lyeth in damnable atheism.' Though some of these comments on the state of affairs around these parishes are not applied to Alvie or to Insh, they indicate something of the condition and influence of the church during these times.

James VI took part in an attempt to appoint 'Protestant bishops' during 1613 – the last Catholic Bishop of Dunkeld was Robert Crichton, appointed in 1571, who, no doubt, tried to assert his authority over Badenoch.

The 'schools in every parish' which John Knox and many of the early Reformers felt to be essential did not happen here, though Kingussie appears in several records as requiring payment for a School Master. Thus in 1642, 1643, 1650, and 1652, Lachlan Grant's appointment as a teacher in Kingussie requiring a salary is mentioned. In 1650 it is Gilbert Hannay, who was still there in 1681. Mr Alexander Brodie was paid between 1701 and 1711, and by the later eighteenth century the school at Kingussie became the first start for many a bright lad from the Western Isles – on their way to 'Studying for the Ministry'. This tradition persisted into our own times. It was the school at Ruthven from which James Macpherson launched his career as the discoverer of the poems of the bard Ossian.

Very often the church was in the doldrums and too many areas either had no minister or one who gave no lead to his people. However the story of the Alvie minister after the battle of Culloden Moor in 1746 shows the leadership which should be given.

William Gordon, Minister of Alvie from 1710 to 1787, gave shelter to two fugitives from the Culloden Moor battle, and later

34

sent them on their way to Lochaber with food and clothing. This was reported to the Hanoverian troops and relayed to their commander. Dr Gordon was arrested and taken to Inverness for trial. The Duke of Cumberland, the commander-in-chief, then aged 24, was attending the trial and Dr Gordon appealed to him. 'My lord,' he said, 'I find myself in a quandary. I am under the direction of two kings' sons. My Heavenly King's Son directs me to shelter the homeless, feed the hungry, clothe the naked. My temporal King's son directs me to turn the hungry and destitute from my door, and hail them to prison... Which should I obey ?'

To Cumberland's credit he commended the Christian principles, and the minister was sent home with gift.

Some months later, in May 1747, Major Donald Stewart, wounded at Culloden, was trying to escape from this closely patrolled district. He came to Alvie manse to seek Dr Gordon's help. Dr Gordon solved the problem by dressing Major Stewart in suitable clothes and as he himself was travelling south to the General Assembly of the Church of Scotland, he took the Major through each check point as his accompanying Elder, a Commissioner to the General Assembly. This story is recounted in the Rev W. Forsyth's book *In the Shadow of Cairngorm*. This suggests that the story was well known locally, though kept from government ears.

By 1780 there was a move to increase the influence of the Church in areas of Scotland which had been most opposed to the Hanoverian government during and after the '45. This move was really aimed to increase the power of the state, and was hardly a help to the promotion of the Gospel. Both Alvie and Insh had their churches rebuilt as 'parliamentary' churches – basically the churches we see now. Though we may regret the thinking behind the rebuilding, we may (and do) rejoice in the existence of the buildings themselves, and fill them with prayer and praise to the glory of God. The Insh and Rothiemurchus manses were also built at this time, to designs of Thomas Telford. (The Insh Manse is now Insh House Guest House.)

Telford in all built 52 churches and 43 manses in the Highlands and Islands of Scotland. We can surmise from this effort by the Westminster Parliament that this area was thought to be dangerously Jacobite.

In 1816 however, Insh church was damp and dark and the Session of Insh appealed to the heritor Sir George Macpherson-Grant who was just celebrating his coming of age. He was pleased to act. The causeway from the east of Loch Insh to the church knoll of Tom Eunan was built and the church repaired. The new manse was built and a worthwhile glebe set up. The glebe at Alvie was never large enough even to keep a cow, though there was a fine walled garden made below the large new manse built in 1810. In that year there were a hundred communicants recorded at the Easter service, which was considered 'satisfactory'. The Sunday gatherings for worship were also of course gatherings of neighbours, who found this the social centre of their week; all news and opinions, gossip and 'hard' news was spread at the weekly gathering at the Kirk. It was common to have the 'crying' of lost cattle and sheep in the kirkyard after the service. In these days of so much mobility, as well as the mass media, it is hard to estimate the importance of the role of the parish gatherings at the kirks, week by week, year by year. Certainly the Kirk held communities together even if Christian teaching did not reach into all hearts.

It must be realised that all through the history of the Reformed Church of Scotland the Kirk Sessions have been the most influential factor in the life of each parish – a greater influence, in many ways, because more constantly present, than the land-owner or clan chief. The elders' function was described (around 1800) as 'both discerning and discouraging the works of darkness – as they should be answerable to God'. This is a very daunting and negative idea; we might today be better served if our elders were to feel that their function was to discover and to encourage the work of the Spirit among the congregation, as they should be answerable to God.

It was the Kirk Session who took issue with the people of the parish about their moral behaviour; reprimands, disciplining and fines were all used as seemed fitting. We may not applaud all the actions taken, but the moral role and stance of the Kirk was made clear. The Kirk Session handled all the problems of poverty — orphans, foundlings, beggars, vagrants, the sick and the lunatic. This continued right up to the passing of the Poor Law of 1845 and beyond. The Session is still the real caring agency in a rural parish. Miss Eliza Grant of Rothiemurchus, the 'Highland Lady' of the wonderful memoirs, writing of Rothiemurchus in the early nineteenth century, recounted that a new minister was 'very learned, but not devout or theological', and that his wife managed the glebe, and the parishioners managed themselves. However the minister could always claim the right of entry into every household to discover and amend the catechising of the children.

Dr Peter Grant, minister of Duthill at that time, was reputed to have had but two sermons; one on Solomon's glory, and one on charity. However Eliza Grant also writes that 'Pastor John', as he was known, of the nearby parish of Abernethy, altered his parish from 'sinners to well-conducted people'. The Highland Lady also remarked that the Shorter Catechism (learnt by most in childhood) and the fairies and myths of the region were all mixed together in people's minds.

The red letter days of baptism, weddings and funeral processions and wakes gave occasions for great gatherings and feastings. Few baptisms took place in Presbyterian or Catholic churches, but rather in people's houses. W.H. Murray, in his biography of Rob Roy Macgregor, gives a splendid picture of Rob Roy's baptism in 1671, and humbler families also used the occasion for celebration and family gatherings. Weddings — of whatever social standing — were naturally also highlights of both town and country life.

There are many good accounts (and pictures) of 'penny weddings' when friends of poorer families organised the collection of a penny from all guests, and the resulting funds were used to provide refreshment — mainly liquid. Though the actual amounts must have been small, the Kirk frowned heavily on the custom, and did its best to prevent such celebrations, especially on the Sabbath. Today, we are perhaps most amazed by the long-drawn out funeral festivities; the Kirk often inveighed against the sometimes chaotic funeral processions and wakes. In 1704 Lachlan Macintosh of Macintosh's funeral involved the family in a month-long period of house-guests, and immense costs for funeral food and drink and furbishings. There is recorded a funeral on the northern edge of Badenoch where the many mourners carrying the coffin to the burying ground, rested it on the parapet of a bridge; while refreshing themselves with the plentifully supplied whisky, they inadvertently pushed the coffin into the river, whereupon it sailed down the Spey in fine style!

The memoirs of the Highland Lady, and the writings of Mrs Grant of Laggan, and others, give us vivid insights into the late eighteenth- and early nineteenth-century life in this area.

Session records both of Alvie and Insh for this period are somewhat bare of detail, but reveal poverty and hunger. There were many bad seasons with poor harvests – November 29th was the date of one 'Harvest Thanksgiving' at Insh. Illness, particularly tuberculosis, and malnutrition, made life-expectancy short. Nonetheless there is plenty of evidence in letters and memoirs of vigour and a spirit which made the people of Badenoch so attractive and remarkable to those who came to visit them and to live among them.

In the late eighteenth and nineteenth centuries ministers of the Church of Scotland were mainly appointed by an uneven system of patronage that produced much resentment among the parishes. One parish, when offered a professor as a minister declared vigorously 'That makes things far waur! He'll just make a bye-job of our souls!' This resentment came to a head in 1840 when the Free Church was born in the movement known as the Disruption. 'Disruption' is just what it was; a division of the people of Scotland which has never been totally healed; a division in terms of property, religious practice, religious understanding, affecting the inner loyalties of the heart. This sad and bitter division affected all parts of Scotland and is shown here by the 'extra' churches we can still see. The scale of the Disruption and of the numbers involved and the amount of money as well as the unhealed rift, shows how deep was the feeling which led to the tragic division. Nowadays the Free Church of Scotland operates from one church in Kingussie; the Roman Catholic presence is still very considerable; the Episcopal Church of Scotland operates here, based on Grantown-on-Spey, with a notable modern church at Inverdruie. The Church of Scotland Presbytery here – the Presbytery of Abernethy – links the parish of Alvie and Insh with its neighbours; Kingussie, Newtonmore and Laggan to the south; Aviemore and Rothiemurchus, Boat of Garten and Carrbridge, Grantown-on-Spey and Dulnain Bridge, as well as Abernethy and Cromdale and Advie, to the north, and also the Moray parishes of Inveravon and Glenlivet, and Tomintoul and Kirkmichael.

We no longer have the great united Communion occasions, such as the mass Communions of 5,000 people at Grantully in Perthshire, or the 9,000 at Uig on the isle of Lewis. Large Communion gatherings did take place. Dalnaspidal, the farm toun near Drumochter pass, visible from the old A9 but not from the new road, used to host several hundred people on a Communion occasion, coming from Calvine, Dalwhinnie, Laggan and Newtonmore and the country round about. Presbytery gatherings do still occur, but rather for the select few than for everyone, but united Christmas celebrations have helped to encourage us. Patterns of worship have changed. Queen Victoria was said to have three rules she wished to impress on visiting clerics; 'Brevity. Brevity. Brevity.' This seems to have had an effect.

The serious matter of who should attend Communion is, I think, well summed up by the minister who said he would 'rather a hundred who should NOT have been at Communion WERE there, than that one would be debarred whom Christ had invited.'

Alvie and Insh parishes have been joined in one parish since August 1931 and they have very slowly come to think of themselves as one parish. This is made easier in the days of the car and the more rapid changes in population. Worship now takes place in three churches; in Insh village in a small refurbished Gospel Hall, in Insh Church above Loch Insh, the oldest site, and in

Alvie Church, seen across Loch Alvie driving south on the old A9. There is also the Badenoch Christian Centre in the village of Kincraig. This was opened by the Church of Scotland in 1976 as a hostel-type Centre where many widely-differing groups may enjoy this marvellous area of Scotland and also, if they wish, meet in Christian fellowship and study and prayer. The Minister of the parish is also the Warden of the Centre, working with a full-time assistant warden. One of the old church halls, now belonging to the Church of Scotland, standing just opposite the Centre, has done excellent duty as a village hall.

All three churches have been altered from their Victorian aspects into light and lovely buildings of simplicity and grace. Those who worship there – and they are many – rejoice in this and in the sense of the continuity of Christian worship here. The influence of the church may perhaps be summed up in this quotation from an old Gaelic prayer collected hereabouts by the Rev Thomas Sinton and published in his 'Songs of the Soul'. Since this prayer was recalled in 1900, it will have been in the minds of many over a long period.

'There is no night that I lie down that the angels of Heaven are not near me, and they seeking me out and preserving me from the enemies that are hot in pursuit.

In my slumber, loving Father, thou art my Shepherd who keepst me alive and who will bring me up to Thy throne when it is thy purpose to take me to Thy glory.'

See Notes 9 and 10, Alvie and Insh Churches, p99 and 100.

5

GOVERNMENT

or – 'Who's in charge here?'

Local tribal leaders gradually agreed to the overlordship of the leaders of larger groupings of tribes. The Caledonii, the group of tribes living in Badenoch and the Moray coastland around 500 AD, accepted the overlordship of the Pictish Kings controlling most of north-east Scotland as well as the Northern Highlands. Finally in 843 AD Kenneth MacAlpine won the prime position, uniting Scotland under one ruler, though the effect on people living in Badenoch is uncertain.

Nowadays the 'overlord' of Badenoch is really the Highland Regional Council, with its headquarters in Inverness, which also governs the whole of the Highlands, as well as Nairn and Caithness. The local District Council is that of Badenoch and Strathspey, a long sausage-shaped area – the northern part from Aviemore to Advie being Strathspey and the southern part, Badenoch – which now covers the area from Lynwilg south to Drumochter and also the western land up the Spey to the end of Loch Laggan. This is probably not so different from the area first recorded in the Moray register of 1229 as 'Badenoch'. (In 1289 it was written Badenagh, Badenoughe; in 1300 Badnasshe; in 1366 Baydebach; in 1467 Badynach; 1539 Baidyenoch; in 1603, from the Huntly register, Badzenoche.)

In the thinking of the Scots of the eleventh century and later, people *used* land rather than owned it; people derived their living from it, drew power from it, and a supply of fighting men, some-times even money. The clan system, of which more hereafter, was based on kinship; the clan chiefs controlled the people and the land, had the power of life and death there, but did not con-sider the ownership of the land theirs as in the feudal system of the Norman south.

As Norman lords came to power-bases in Scotland (Comyns,

Bruces, Randolphs...), a good deal of feudalism came too, though this hardly penetrated the Highlands. The confusion of the two systems in people's minds leads to confusion to this day.

Early records of what happened here are few. Early buildings were easily destroyed by fire. Stone buildings were expensive luxuries, and even these used timber in their interiors; churches, monasteries castles and town buildings were all frequently burnt out, so we are lucky if any records, registers or accounts survive. Many records were also 'lost', including those of the twentieth century. We do know that in 1364 the Bishop of Moray was invested with the powers of Justiciary within the districts of Strathspey and Badenoch which later became a barony and not a church property. Badenoch had become part of the Moray lands some time before 1190, but it is a long way from Elgin and Huntly, not rich in any way, either in men or goods, so that neither church nor overlords troubled very much about it.

Since Badenoch was remote and difficult to get at, control was limited and it probably made little difference to the folk living here when after 1212 the Comyns thought they were firmly in control. They held great lands in Moray and Buchan, but finally lost them as they lost the fight against the Bruce. In 1371 the lordship belonged to a younger son of Robert II, Alexander Stewart, better known as 'the Wolf of Badenoch', and he did have an impact here. He died in 1406 and is buried in Dunkeld Cathedral, and all the stories about him are horrific. Apart from burning Elgin Cathedral in 1390 (and with it many records of all kinds – church monastic, legal, family – a great and irreparable loss) the Wolf ruled his lands and his people cruelly, using his powers of life and death ruthlessly, burning the homes of those who displeased him, extorting labour as well as goods beyond reason. He reinforced and extended his castles at Lochindorb and Loch-an-Eilean, and strengthened the castle at Ruthven; however he made little change to Castle Roy at Nethy Bridge whose walls still stand, showing us one of the older castle designs of Scotland.

There was altogether a fearful lack of law, of order, of peace, in early medieval Scotland which persisted far too long under a series of kings who were either minors or weakened in some way. The brief remaining chronicle of 1398 in the register of Moray says 'in those days there was no law in Scotland, but the strong oppressed the weak, and the whole kingdom was a den of thieves. Homicides, robberies, fire-raisings and other evil deeds went unpunished, and justice was outlawed, was in exile beyond the bounds of the kingdom.' In any remaining register of rents or tribute from many places there can too frequently be read one word – 'wast'.

If the fourteenth century seems to have been a time of anarchy, the fifteenth and sixteenth centuries were little better, and indeed are sometimes referred to as 'the age of forays'. (There is a penetrating account of this time in *Periods in Highland History* by I.F. Grant and Hugh Cheape.) Clans were developing into larger and stronger entities and the struggle for the control of lands increased, both among clan leaders and between those leaders and the crown.

The clan system of Scotland, the ancient social system of the Highlands, developed from the early days of the fusing of the Pictish and Scottish races, and was only slightly modified by the influx of the Norman nobles bringing the feudal ideas of England into parts of Scotland. These ideas did not really ever apply to the Highland areas.

Thus here the laws of inheritance, land tenure, office tenure, marriage and succession are Scottish. Gaeldom – Alba, the Highlands, and in the end the Islands too, together with the Borders and the rich Central belt – gradually became the nation of Scotland as the central monarchy developed. There gradually assimilated into one unit the English, Norse, Pictish and Dalriadic elements of which Scotland was formed, but naturally each area retained more of one element than of others.

In Scots society the clan system, though sometimes appearing almost 'feudal' in the English sense, rests on the idea that the lowliest 'working peasant' was of the same blood as the Chief, was his brother, cousin, or kin. This Scots pattern, so different from the English hierarchical feudalism, thus formed a non-class tribal society, even though dues and tenure were parts of it.

Feuds were, unhappily, very much part of this system of intense loyalties, with the resulting destruction of life, property and peace of mind. As an illustration of the attitude to feuds and their settlement we can take the celebrated 'Battle of the Inches' fought on the North Inch of Perth in 1396. This was a 'judicial combat' in which people of Badenoch were involved; thirty members of Clan Chattan were to fight thirty members of Clan Kay (Davidsons). The Perth town exchequer records show accounts listing the expenditure of £14.2s.11d. 'for wood and iron making the enclosure for 60 persons fighting on the Inch of Perth.'

Of the 60, seven of Clan Chattan survived though wounded, and two of the Davidsons, and one Davidson was 'unaccounted for.'

The grave of one of the survivors of the battle, Fergus Shaw, is to be found in the old kirkyard of Rothiemurchus. He died in 1405, the last of the Shaws to hold power in the district. The legends about him have multiplied, and their existence shows what a dynamic man the survivor of so much violence must have been, in that age so full of feuds and bloodshed. It is noted that the word 'clan' was first used of the Grants during the lifetime of Sir John Grant, c1475.

In general it seems that the people of Badenoch had to concentrate on surviving. The local dues of rents, services, and support for fighting and reiving forays were under the control of the local laird, chieftain or chief, until well into the eighteenth century, persisting, as here in Badenoch, right up to the destruction of the system after the '45. Even then central control was difficult to establish. The lifestyle of the Highlands can be deduced from the ways in which they continued to meet the demands for rent and tribute (taxes). Butter, cheese, oatmeal, barley, and sometimes malt, cattle, pigs, eels, salmon and venison were all used in payment, as well as manual service on the land.

The recurrent eclipse of the power of the crown due to the youth or absence of the sovereign meant that during the 14th, 15th, and 16th centuries the local leaders increased their power, and clan leaders regarded themselves as almost above the law.

The Crown did manage to reduce the almost sovereign powers of the Lords of the Isles (c1493) and then used Campbells and Mackenzies as their allies to the detriment of the smaller clans. Dr I.F. Grant writes of 'the law of the jungle' operating in the Highlands in the sixteenth century.

For a clan that did not co-operate with the royal power and its agent, punishment was usually inflicted by a grant of 'Letters of Fire and Sword' to whichever clan claimed to be most damaged. This clan was then legally empowered to act against their enemies. A proclamation of this kind was sent by the crown in 1528 to the sheriffdoms of the North-East and to 'leading noble families, barons, captains and gentlemen in their bounds' to proceed against Clan Chattan and 'invaid them to thair uter destruction, by slauchter, byrning, drowning and uther wayis...' 'to let no creatur levand of that clann, except preistis, women and bairns.' Though this order was carried out by the Earl of Moray to some extent, it is good to know that the Macintoshes eventually were able to resume occupation of the lands of Badenoch. The lands of Dunachton became secure to the Macintosh from the Earl of Moray in 1624.

No clan chief could really provide protection for his clansmen but this period of uncertainty and fighting resulted in bonds of great strength being forged within the clans and immense loyalty to the chiefs became a real force in the Highlands. In the late seventeenth century in the Grant lands of Strathspey it became popular to take the name of Grant in addition to a patronym or place name, as Davidsons, within Clan Chattan, adopted the name Macpherson. Dr Grant writes that 'even at the end of the seventeenth century it was customary for the clansmen to pray for their chief when they said grace.'

The development of the clans into fighting forces gave rise to the music of the bagpipes as we now know it. The pipes gave the music which stirred and gathered the fighting forces into an effective weapon – as they still do. The old music of the clarsach, the ballads, remained the treasure source of the great deeds of the past, recreating, enhancing and preserving our heritage of song and story; but the pipes were needed to inspire and activate the larger bodies of men used in the wars of the later centuries. The wars themselves became larger in scale, greater areas and more men being affected. A chief would have his personal piper, such as 'The Laird of Grant's Piper' whose portrait by Richard Waitts can be seen in the National Museum of Scotland.

Pipe music is an immense study in itself, but Badenoch can claim Calum Macpherson (1828–1898), piper to Cluny, of Cat Lodge by Laggan, 'Calum Piobair – easily the best player of piobraireachd I have ever heard' and 'one of the greatest exponents of the Macrimmon tradition,' whose tradition reaches down to our own late-twentieth-century times, with John MacDougall of Kincraig, a champion piper and teacher. (See Note 11, The Piper's Memorial, p103.)

It is difficult to assess clan control of people or areas. Dr I.F. Grant writes that though the first Shaw had an indefinite title to lands around Inverness and the Laigh of Moray, his descendants, known as 'Sons of the Chief' – 'Mac an Toisich ' – developed into Clan Macintosh and made a pact with MacBeans and MacGillivrays. A later descendant, claiming to be chief of Clan Chattan was opposed by some, including those descended from a churchman of Kingussie, who formed the clan MacPherson.

All these – Macintoshes, MacBeans, MacGillivrays, Macphersons – held title not from the crown but from other chiefs – here mainly from Huntly, Chief of the Gordons. (See Note 12, Clan Chattan, p104.) Certain Anglo-Norman families taking hold of land in the Highland area grew into clans. John Grant took over land in Strathspey in 1434, and by 1538 the Grants are accepted as a clan. By 1600 the Highlands were more or less controlled by clans holding accepted power over accepted areas. Fortified castles denoted the land-bases; Roy Castle at Nethybridge, the castles on Lochindorb and on Loch-an Eilean, and at Ruthven, were the strongholds to which hard-pressed forces could retreat. They did not develop into fortified houses; Raitts Castle vanished and the dwelling house of Balavil replaced it. Dunachton was never properly rebuilt after its burning in 1689, until its nineteenth-century rebuilding as a shooting lodge. Dunachton was however the power-base and residence of the Macintosh of Macintosh during the sixteenth and seventeenth centuries, the base from which cattle reiving was directed. The traces of this part of our history around us are few. The old clan names survive; place names indicate mills, ferries, sheep fanks, and there is a hill on the south bank of the Feshie known as the 'Queen's Snout' which, by tradition, is the hill from which the agents of Mary, Queen of Scots (probably Gordons, under Huntly's orders) stood and watched the Ruthven lands being 'put to the torch', about 1562. The Queen herself never penetrated here. How much damage was done to the houses, steadings, stock, or crops, is not recorded but the event cannot have endeared the Crown or the Gordons to the people of these parts.

The clan government of this area, as in other parts of the Highlands, was put under pressure by the attempts of James VI to develop and enforce the power of the Crown, but there is no evidence of his edicts ever having any effect on Badenoch. James VI suffered from many misconceptions which were very damaging to his kingdoms. He believed that the land of the Highlands was rich and fertile and therefore should be heavily taxed; also that the people of the Highlands were 'suche wilde savages void of Godis feare and obedience'. They were 'Barbarous for the most part'. He seems to have hated the Islanders even more, for he actually put on paper an order which Huntly undertook to perform, for the 'extirpation of the Barbarous people of the Yllis within a year'. The Statutes of Iona of 1609, if enforced, would have destroyed the Highland system even earlier than actually happened.

These Statutes, punitive as they were, were an attempt to increase royal power through the Church. Chiefs were to enforce obedience to ministers; to see that stipends were paid (Charles I, James' son made a better attempt to arrange this, for which he got small thanks from the developing Presbyterian church) the repair of the kirk buildings was to be supervised by the chiefs; also the observance of the Sabbath and the 'exercise of discipline'. However these statutes were never operative, since civil war and the reclaiming efforts of the Roman Catholic missionary priests, the absence of any strong royal power meant that most places went on as they were, and this would be true of Badenoch also.

The Reformation established the Kirk's power in the parishes rather than the royal power, but the clan chiefs remained the real force locally until their destruction after 1745.

6

DOCTRINES AND DIVISIONS

Campaigns and Counter-Marches

The great events of history in Scotland between 1550 and 1700 – that is the Reformation, the establishment of the Presbyterian Church, the union of the Crown with that of England, and the later risings in favour of the Stuart line of monarchs, with all the confused and tragic events which stemmed from them – affected Badenoch indeed, but much less than most other parts of Scotland. During the ferocities of the Bishops' Wars, under Charles I, the Civil Wars, when Cromwell invaded Scotland, and during the Covenanters' bitter fighting against royal authority, Badenoch was only on the fringes of the conflicts.

The Reformation was the major effort to destroy the corruption and faults which had developed within the Church in western Europe. It is true that the church in the sixteenth century had many faults and that reform was urgently needed. The Counter Reformation was the movement within the Roman Catholic Church which worked to put things right without division. The Reformation can be described as the change from the Roman Catholic system of religious thought and management, built on the dominant position of the Pope, the Bishop of Rome, and all bishops under him, to the Protestant system, in which the individual approached God and the Bible in his own right without the intermediary of a priest, and sought for himself the truths of the Christian faith. The government and organisation of Protestant churches throughout Europe was developed in very varied forms. (There are, of course, many more differences between Catholic and Protestant and many similarities too.)

The government of the church in Scotland changed from rule

from Rome through the authority of archbishops, bishops and priests, to the control of the Kirk in Scotland by a group of priests or presbyters, resulting in 'Presbyterianism'. This meant that the 'oversight' of the Kirk's affairs was run by Presbyteries, local groupings of presbyters or priests who saw to it that a more disciplined, yet individualistic, form of prayer and teaching and worship was instituted and maintained. Kirk Sessions were formed in each parish and became powerful forces in the life of the Kirk throughout Scotland, and indeed in everyone's lives.

As these different teachings touched men's very hearts, they were vigorously expounded and were the cause of much division and resultant hatred, violence, fear and unhappiness, the very reverse of the society Christ's Church should build.

Political divisions, largely based on religious differences also damaged lives everywhere, including Badenoch. James VI (James I of England) believed – as so many did – that God had divinely appointed the rule of Kings and that rebellion was therefore sin. When the Reformers taught rule by Presbyteries and not by Bishops, King James was to exclaim 'I see what you want – no bishop – no king!' [ie local control by self-appointed groups of clergy, not by royally appointed bishops, which logically led to Parliamentary rule not royal government]. This line of thought led to the Bishops' Wars under Charles I, the Civil War and the Covenanters' Wars. To most Scots the Stuarts were their rightful kings, but when a Stuart monarch, James VII and II, became a Roman Catholic, with a Catholic heir, many folk both sides of the Border, wanted to change to a Protestant King. They also wanted to increase the power of Parliament and decrease the power of the Crown. This political doctrine was as divisive as the religious doctrines. Thus the doctrines and divisions in people's loyalties, their hearts and minds, led to the campaigns which shattered the peace of Europe and of England and Scotland too. The campaigns, often of small forces moving rapidly, increased the ravages of famine and foul weather wherever and whenever the warring troops passed.

In 1645 when James Graham, Marquis of Montrose, led his magnificent but finally disastrous campaigns for the Royalist cause, the impact on the Highlands was considerable, but here Montrose's marches and manoeuvres only touched a small part of our area. The number of Badenoch men concerned in his campaigns was possibly about 300, listed as 'men from Badenoch, mainly Gordons, Keppochs, and Macdonalds armed with pike and claymore.'

The story of Montrose's fight for the Crown must begin with his declaration that he called men to arms 'for the defence and maintenance of the true Protestant religion, his Majesty's just and sacred authority, the fundamental laws and privileges of Parliament and freedom of the oppressed and enthralled subject'; and with his statement of faith in the King: 'Knew I not perfectly his Majesty's intentions to be such, and so real as is already expressed, I should never have embarked myself at all in his service.' The military account of these campaigns is brilliantly recounted in John Buchan's biography of Montrose; Buchan writes: 'Two followers, four sorry horses, little money and no baggage seems a slender outfit for the conquest of a kingdom; but in six months he had Scotland at his feet.'

At Blair Atholl Montrose linked up with 'Colkitto', Alistair Macdonald, that brilliant and charismatic leader who with his Irish forces was fighting for the king in the south of Scotland, and the campaign began. The first serious fighting was at Tippermuir, south of Perth, where the battle was an outstanding victory for the King's ragged army. Montrose's losses were few and his discipline strong so that he was able to make maximum use of his victory. The refurbishment of his forces taken from the 'fair city of Perth' was very great... it was very much needed. The following whirlwind campaign through Fife and Aberdeenshire was successful, though discipline did break down at Aberdeen where there was some looting and slaughter. Montrose pulled his men rapidly out of the town, moving quickly north by way of Strathavon and Tomintoul, coming down to rest at Rothiemurchus. He used the castle on Loch-an-Eilean (originally built by the Wolf of Badenoch, and owned successively by Shaws, Macintoshes and Grants), and then moved on further south up the Spey. Alistair Macdonald –

Colkitto – at this juncture went west with his own forces to raise recruits from Clan Donald. Montrose was thus left with only 500 men and needed to revise his plans.

Here in Badenoch, at Invereshie, at this time, Montrose was seriously ill; he was even thought to be dead and the Covenanters began to give thanks to the Almighty! But by October 4th Montrose left Badenoch for Atholl and led his small army rapidly round Scotland, with Argyll's forces following seven or eight days behind – not easy for those living in the path of the troops. In November Montrose led his men through the 'Badenoch passes' (Gaick ?? Minigaig ?? Drumochter ??) and then down to Blair and Dunkeld. At Blair he met Colkitto who had returned with a strong muster of western clans. It was on December 11th that the lightning strikes on the Campbells were launched. Montrose went west by Rannoch and into the hills to disguise his movements and then made the devastating attacks on Argyll's forces at Inverary and Inverlochy.

Montrose wrote to the King : '…that through God's blessing, I am in the fairest hopes of reducing this kingdom to your Majesty's obedience.' Marches and counter-marches from the west to Dundee, to the hills, to the coasts, culminated in the battles of Auldearn and Alford, where the armies of the Covenanters were destroyed. By August Montrose was master of Scotland.

But elsewhere 'the King's Crown had gone down'; defeated at Naseby, Charles I's fortunes never recovered. Montrose's campaigns never crossed Badenoch again; his defeat, betrayal and capture, his execution, the triumph of the King's enemies must have been felt here where the loyalty of the area was with the King. We can only surmise the effect of these campaigns on the families of Badenoch. We do not know the casualties, the loss of goods and gear, nor the effect of the lack of menfolk to work this difficult land.

When the Commonwealth was set up after the defeat and execution of Charles I (1649) and under the Lords of Convention, who with their generals were the real power in the land, Scotland was not a flourishing country, though Badenoch was spared many of the trials of the Lowlands. Under Charles II it was little better and Lauderdale, the King's chief minister, had a terrible reputation among the people.

Though it is far from the centres of government, cut off from the centres of population, the events known in England as the 'Glorious Revolution' (despite the slaughter of Sedgemoor, and the Bloody Assizes) caused chaos here in Badenoch, and lasting damage.

Charles II's successor, James II and VII, the last Stuart king, was accepted by the clans as their king to whom they were bound by a loyalty from which only the king himself could release them. When the Catholic James lost control of the situation in the south and south-west of England, the people of Britain had to choose between James, the lawful King, a Roman Catholic with Roman Catholic heir to the throne, and William of Orange, himself half Stuart, but a Protestant, together with his wife Mary, James' daughter and a Protestant. William was quickly the 'de facto' king of England and soon King by law. Scotland took longer to decide and the decision proved to be more costly especially in the Highlands.

The Highlanders were mainly on the Stuart side, while the Covenanting Lowlanders and the population of the Central and Eastern lowlands backed the 'government' side under William.

At the calling of a 'Convention Parliament' John Graham, Viscount Claverhouse and Dundee, declared his continued support for James VII and II, his friend and master. The old song, to the cavalry canter tune of 'Bonnie Dundee', has it rightly :

'To the Lords of Convention 'twas Claverhouse spoke.
Ere the King's crown go down there are crowns to be broke;
Then tremble, false Whigs in the midst of your glee
For you've no' seen the last of my Bonnets and me!'

The rest of the song goes on to describe what Dundee really did do; having left Edinburgh with a fair body of men, he failed to get into Stirling, so then rode north for Dundee. He and his troops were not welcomed by the City Fathers so Dundee raised the King's Standard on Dundee Law with a fine show of military bravado.

There followed a 'round Scotland campaign' of swift marches and near interceptions of the two forces, under Dundee and under Sir Hugh Mackay of Scourie, the government commander. Marching up the east coast from Dundee, via Huntly, Elgin and Forres, Dundee reached Inverness, having out-marched and out-witted Mackay. Unfortunately Dundee found Macdonald of Keppoch burning and looting the town, offending the townspeople and the MacIntosh of MacIntosh, both nominally on the King's side. Having stopped this, but finding his troops fewer, Dundee led his remaining forces rapidly down Loch Ness and crossed the hills between the end of Loch Ness and the Spey. He crossed the Spey itself by the fords opposite Cluny Castle. The Cluny of the day was a great fence sitter, but his clan were 'keen and hearty' for the king. From this friendly countryside Dundee sent out a 'Royal Letter' (as previously arranged with James) calling all the faithful clans, 'bidding them be ready with their men by the Kalends of May' (May 18th).

On May 10th Dundee moved his forces from Cluny Castle to Blair Castle, and followed this with successful and unexpected attacks on Dunkeld and Perth, then moving across the Sidlaws to Dundee. By this time the government forces were alarmed and depressed and almost totally disrupted. Still getting no support from Dundee's Provost ('douce man'!) the king's forces moved rapidly west to rejoin the clans who should have been gathering. Dundee reached Glen Spean and the shores of Loch Lochy after an unnecessarily exhausting march across Rannoch Moor. There he joined forces with Lochiel who re-provisioned him and they established a base in Glen Roy. From there the 'Fiery Cross' was sent out to all the clans. This traditional signal, of 'a spear crossed with two wooden javelins dipped in pitch and set blazing' was carried north, east and west from Lochaber. The clans responded.

The number of fighting men a clan could muster was the sign of its power, the real indication of the strength and influence of a clan. (To estimate the possibility of another rebellion after the

'45, an English survey was secretly made on this basis – the last measurement of the clan system ever made.)

By May 18th the clans assembled; Lochiel brought about 400 men; Glengarry, 300; 100 Macdonalds came from Glencoe; 200 Stewarts of Appin came; 200 Keppoch Macdonalds; there were Macdonalds of Sleat, Macleans of Morven, Macneills of Barra, Macleods of Raasay, Macgregors, and many men of Badenoch, MacIntoshes, MacPhersons, MacGillivrays, Grants, Shaws, and Davidsons. On May 28th this army, pipers, buglers, drummers, with camp followers and provision wagons and pack ponies, marched out of Glen Roy by Garva More and down the Spey to camp that night at Raitts Castle.

Dundee managed to maintain some discipline over his army but the effect of this major movement of men on the countryside here, and on the food supplies far and wide, was tremendous, especially on countryside as poor as this. May 29th was a day of celebration – Charles II's birthday. Dundee addressed the clan chiefs, in order to inspire them with increased loyalty to the royal cause, lit a bonfire, proposed a health to King James and his triumphant return to his kingdom.

Across the Spey the Government forces in Ruthven Castle, under a Captain Forbes, with a contingent of Grants, watched to see what this great assembly of fighting men might do. No word had come from General Mackay, who was thought to be somewhere south of Inverness. As the first call to surrender was refused by Forbes, Keppoch and his men began to fill the moat with brushwood; Forbes, still having had no word of Mackay's approach, agreed to surrender, and he and his men marched out unharmed, northwards across the moor of Feshie. Dundee then gave Keppoch the order to fire the castle, which was done most successfully.

From the coming of the Fiery Cross, all the movements of the king's forces, as well as those of the government troops, would have been made visible to the local people by the camp fires lit, the torches moving – and the conflagration of Ruthven would have told its own story. No doubt the men of Badenoch found opportunity to get back to their own homes while the main force was at Raitts Castle; some would have seen Captain Forbes and his men crossing the Tromie and the Feshie on their way to find General Mackay.

Mackay heard of all these movements when he was just south of Inverness and decided not to retreat but to march rapidly south up the Spey to cut Dundee's Highlanders off from the Gordon forces in the east. Dundee meanwhile was moving some of his forces north as fast as he could, to try to catch Mackay unprepared. Moving from his base at Raitts towards Loch Alvie, he was passing Dunachton, when Keppoch, as insubordinate as usual, set fire to the castle, alleging that he thought the Macintosh an enemy of King James. Dundee rebuked him sternly and he promised no further acts of disobedience, but the damage was done; divisions among the clans, such as this, often led to men leaving the force, to internal fighting, to unnecessary depletion and destruction of precious stores. Areas were usually left in chaos and distress by passing troops, with very seldom any compensation.

By Loch Alvie, some dragoons led by a Captain Alexander Bruce found a reardguard detachment of Mackay's troops. Shouted contact was made – Bruce suggesting that the rearguard changed sides! – but the reply was a fusillade of shots and a hurried departure. The pursuit continued past Castle Grant, up the river Livet to Edinglassie, but Dundee could not make contact with Mackay, so called off the pursuit, burning down Edinglassie and all its stores which he could not carry away.

With both armies trying to catch the other off guard, they nearly met close to the Boat of Garten, when a minor skirmish filled the air with smoke. Dundee led his troopers into the action, but Mackay's dragoons broke off the engagement and withdrew to the main forces. The clansmen lifted the plunder from the enemy's camp, which initially encouraged them, but then, as so often, vanished from the army to take their booty home. However new clans were still coming in with fighting men and Dundee decided to cross Badenoch to his old quarters at Glen Roy, where he settled on June 11th.

Food was becoming very scarce and difficult to obtain, though

Lochiel had promised the resources of Lochaber 'to the last cow'. There was all the disruption caused by the passing and re-passing of two armies and in addition though summer had come there had been two particularly hard winters in 1687 and 1688. There was little grazing even in June. It is hard to realise nowadays the difficulties of living when no outside supplies are available. Those who deal with livestock will recognise some of the problems: lambs die in hard springs, cows are thin and milkless... it is amazing that the men were fit to fight, and terrible to think of the hardships and hunger of the people left after the armies had passed.

Macpherson of Cluny never gave Dundee his full support and it is possible that not all the men of fighting age in Badenoch were swept into Dundee's army. Those who met Dundee himself were often inspired to follow him; his 'mystique', the something that has kept him the 'Bonnie Dundee' of legend and overrode his reputation as 'Bluidy Claverhouse', certainly added men to the King's banner, both in Badenoch and Atholl where the men were for him while Atholl himself was opposed.

This was effectively the last month of the war. By a letter to Cluny of July 18th, Dundee told him to have his men ready to join him on July 22nd; the letter also concludes an agreement for provisions to be supplied to the army. So on July 22nd, nearly 2,000 men left Glen Roy, skirting Loch Laggan and then turning south to march down the Garry on the way to Blair Castle. It was reported that morale was high.

By July 26th they were south of Blair Castle, just north of the Pass of Killiecrankie. (A standing stone, in a field east of the old A9, marks Dundee's command post.) The battle of Killiecrankie was fought on July 27th. This was a great victory for the Highlanders and a very comprehensive defeat for the government forces. Mackay's army lost more than a third of its number and many prisoners were taken as well. The King's forces lost far fewer, but whereas Mackay lost only three officers, many of the Highland officers were killed. Most seriously, Dundee himself was killed in the early stages of the battle. (It is said that he was killed by a silver bullet, piercing his cuirass; his power was thought not to be susceptible to an ordinary bullet.)

The Highland charges which swept the opposing troops aside, pushing many into the ravines of the Garry, were awesome, magnificent, overpowering, and as effective in this battle as on any occasion, but the loss of the leaders nullified the success the charges had won. The loss of Dundee was disastrous for his cause, for the Highlands and for its people. (In the 1719 Jacobite campaign, amid military mismanagement, an officer was heard to exclaim 'Oh for an hour of Dundee!') Though the government was most alarmed, and Mackay, with his army and all communications totally disrupted, expected to be destroyed by the pursuit, the King's army never regained any cohesion or enthusiasm. After a costly and indecisive attack on Dunkeld on August 21st, the clans dispersed – back to their glens for the harvest. They did not gather again in any numbers till the following year when under Major-General Thomas Buchan they were bloodily defeated above the Spey on the Haughs of Cromdale. Few of the men who left Badenoch that time returned.

Worse for the clans than even the loss of their men, was the government attitude to the Highlanders. Some of William's government reckoned it was wiser to exterminate the wild men of the hills. Sir John Dalrymple, Earl of Stair, proposed such a scheme; an outcome of this thinking was the bloody and treacherous massacre of the MacDonalds of Glencoe in 1692. No wonder that the Highlanders felt little loyalty to the Government, nor any enthusiasm for the Act of Union of 1707, uniting the Parliaments of Scotland and England.

7
TIMES OF CHANGE
1690–1790

'Treason doth never prosper; what's the reason ?
If it do prosper none dare call it treason.'
Anon, 17th century

This cynical rhyme is perhaps a useful insight into the politics of eighteenth-century Britain; maybe it is especially true in the Highlands. The hundred years following 1690 saw very many changes in every part of the lives of the people living here, not least in their loyalties. The acceptance of the Government of William and Mary led on to the Act of Union in 1707, under Queen Anne, James VII's second daughter, when Scotland and England became one country. It is probable that the changes that Act brought to Badenoch were minimal – perhaps just mental confusion; however it did not endear Queen Anne's government to the Highlands.

One of the drawbacks which Scotland suffered after William's successful usurpation of the throne was that, while perhaps naturally, he relied on his own countrymen as his chief advisors, a Dutchman was not likely to know or care what happened north of the Highland line. The leaders of William's government were intent on establishing a smooth-running, well-financed country whose foreign policy and money would promote the commercial (and so imperial) interests of England, and of William's own beloved Netherlands. Both these countries were combating the growing power of France,

In England, the challenge to the crown's power – demonstrated by the overthrow of James II and VII – was really based on Parliament. In the Highlands it was still based on the powerful nobles and clan leaders.

In Badenoch the clans were small in size, and so not powerful;

Gordons and Campbells were the great mainland clans. In Badenoch Clan Chattan men held to the Gordons against the Campbells, and thus with the MacDonalds. The terrible years after Killiecrankie, when hard winters and famine added to the distress in Badenoch, saw many die of disease and more of hunger. The agricultural reforms which gradually infiltrated here were possibly made easier because past practices, as well as land once tilled, had dropped out of use with the fall in the population.

Dr I.F. Grant has published a wonderful book, *Everyday Life on an old Highland Farm*, in which she records and analyses the details of farm life at Dunachton, as revealed by the account books of William Macintosh of Balnespick, between the years 1769 and 1782. (They also throw light on the years before and after those dates.) Studying Dr Grant's book we can gain an excellent picture of life in this parish. It is particularly remarkable because the early and mid-eighteenth century was the time of the Jacobite risings and while it is possible to gain from this book a detailed picture of the way of life here and hereabouts through these traumatic years, the account books do not give any indication of the effect of the campaigns of 1715, 1719, or 1745–46, or even that they happened.

In 1715, however, the Macintosh of Macintosh called up 600 men to rally to the Stuart cause and the risings really did effect the lives of all in Badenoch. Also the agricultural changes of this time, as well as the development of woollen and cotton mills, meant that throughout Scotland the patterns of living changed, though slowly, so that the end of the eighteenth century saw a very different society from that of 1690. This was true of Badenoch also.

This period saw three main attempts to restore the Stuart monarchy, in 1715, 1719, and the final tragedy of 1745–46. This was a time of disaster for Scotland no matter to which side loyalty was given. The earlier campaigns took place far from Badenoch, though the effects were felt here. In 1718 the Hanoverian government built Ruthven Barracks on the site of the earlier castles, as another strong point on the new roads then being built. The great road over the Corrieyairack Pass led to the construction of the barracks at Garva More – the 'King's House' – so that the road to Inverness and the road from Fort Augustus could be patrolled.

People of this area were involved in the risings; there is no exact record of numbers, and few lists of names, but James Macintosh, the younger brother of Balnespick, was 'out' in the '15, suffering capture, imprisonment, fines and transportation, finally coming home broken in health and fortunes. The younger Brigadier Macintosh of Raitts became embroiled in intrigues to raise money and men, and was also 'out' in the '15. He too was captured, but escaped, got back to Raitts, only to be re-captured later. Balnespick himself was never 'out', but it cannot have been an easy time for any one. Macintosh of Macintosh never declared for the Stuarts, but his wife 'Colonel Anne' did, and was indeed an effective agent for the Prince.

It was in July 1745 that Prince Charles Edward landed in Scotland to win the kingdom for his father, King James VIII and III.

'Go home', said the old chief at Glenfinnan; 'I am come home', replied the young Prince. A reward was offered by George II for anyone who would capture the 'Young Pretender'; Prince Charles Edward offered a similar reward to any who would seize the 'Elector of Hanover'. These fine words perhaps confuse us as to the risks that so many were taking; the campaigns of the '45 were always a gamble. Many families sat on the fence; many families had members active on opposing sides. It must be remembered too that for many it was not a matter for choice; it was not a rebellion but a legitimate move to expel an illegitimate government. The campaigns and movements are all well documented; the real loyalties of many are hard to gauge. Economically it was always a disaster to everyone; to the clans in the Highlands it led to extinction.

The wretched rain-sodden gallant and ghastly battle on Culloden Moor on April 16th 1746 was 'the end of an old song'.

There are indeed many Jacobite songs, some more romantic and sentimental than others, but it is never possible to disregard totally such a strong body of tradition. Principal Shairp summed up widely held feelings when he wrote this ballad nearly a hundred years later (See Note 13, Principal Shairp, p106).

Culloden Muir
The moorland wide and waste and brown
Heaves far and near and up and down,
Few trenches green the desert crown,
And these are the graves of Culloden.

Here Camerons clove the red line through.
There Stewarts dared what man can do,
Charged lads of Atholl, staunch and true,
To the cannon's mouths on Culloden.

What boots it now to point and tell,
Here the Clan Chattan bore them well;
Shame-maddened, yonder Keppoch fell,
Lavish of life, on Culloden?

Now strangers come to pry and peep
Above the mounds where clansmen sleep,
But what do we, their kinsmen, reap
For our sires' blood shed on Culloden?

Our small farms turned to deserts dumb,
Where smoke no homes, no people come,
Save English hunters, – that's the sum
Of what we have reaped for Culloden.
O the desolate moor of Culloden.

For Badenoch the shape of things to come – military control – was shown in the rebuilding and garrisoning of Ruthven Castle as a government barracks in 1718 (we can see the shell of this today) and of the King's House barracks at Garva More, as well as in the building of the new roads and bridges, surveyed by Burt and constructed under General Wade and General Caulfield from the 1720s to the 1740s.

The outbreak of the fighting – the first contact between the armies – was August 11th 1745 when the Prince's forces came south from Inverness, down the Great Glen, and over from Fort Augustus by the fine new road over the Corrieyairack. Cope's army was fleeing in front of them and some deserters turning back to join the Prince were encountered on the remarkable descending zig-zags of the pass. The mood of the Jacobite army was enthusiastic and Badenoch men joined too.

Ruthven, like the other forts or barracks put up along the new roads, was inadequately garrisoned. However the command was held by an Irishman Sergeant Malloy, whose remarkable story is revealed in a letter to his superior officer, and this letter is still extant. It reads thus:

'Honoured general. This to acquaint you that yesterday there appeared in the little town of Ruthven, above 300 men of the enemy and sent proposals to me that I should surrender. My answer was that I was too old a soldier to surrender a garrison without bloody noses. They threatened hanging me and my men for refusal. I told them I would take my chance. This morning they attacked me at 12 o'clock (midnight) with 150 men. They attacked foregate and sallypoint and attempted to set sallypoint on fire with some old barrels. They drew off about half an hour after 3. There are two men dead of their wounds in the town and three more they took with them. I lost one man shot through the head by foolishly holding his head too high over the parapet. I expect another visit this night but I shall give them the warmest reception my weak party can afford. I shall hold out as long as possible.'

The attack does not seem to have been renewed, and Sergeant Malloy was able to withdraw his small garrison without loss; the Jacobite forces burnt the roof off the barracks and never made use of them.

The Prince's army reached Perth unopposed, and there the

Prince's stirring proclamation drew more support. 'You may rest assured that I put my faith in no other arm than the justice of my cause and in the justice and affection of my people.' Proclaiming his father King, the Prince swept on to Edinburgh, and the victory at Prestonpans. By the end of October the Jacobites had a force of 4,500 infantry and 500 horse, and started for the invasion of England.

Much has been written of the history of the months between that October and the following April. The allegations of incompetence (on both sides), the bad advice, bad faith, and even treachery, are numerous and conflicting. The Jacobite army reached Derby on December 4th. The retreat began on December 6th. We do not know how many Badenoch men were still with the Prince by then, but for everyone the retreat was dire. The good Jacobite victory at Falkirk in February could not restore morale, and it does seem that the Prince received particularly inept and conflicting advice at this time.

There was a local victory, known as 'the Rout of Moy', on April 14th. The Prince's army was camped at Moy, and the Hanoverian army, based on Inverness, got news of this and sent 1,500 men under Lord Loudon, to take the Prince by surprise. However word of this plan was secretly sent to Moy. As Loudon's men struggled up the track, where the new A9 now runs, a small party of local lads and old men, led by the blacksmith of Moy, (the main Macintosh force was actually with the main army) so shouted, whistled, gave mythical orders, moved torches behind peat stacks, and gave the impression of a large, alert body of men, that Lord Loudon and his men, alarmed, turned back and retreated to Inverness.

General Wade, aged 73, had been superseded by George II's son, the Duke of Cumberland, aged 24, and though he was no general, he was ruthless and feared; in addition he had more trained troops and more artillery. There were confused and exhausting marches and counter-marches (attested by several memoirs, including the bitter words of Lord Elcho), which culminated in the two armies coming face to face on April 16th on Culloden Moor.

The Cairngorms (*Photo*: David Hayes)

Looking east across the Spey towards Ruthven from Creag Dhu (*Photo:* David Hayes)

Ruthven Barracks from the north (*Photo:* David Hayes)

Glen Fleshie
(*Photo:* David Hayes)

Loch-an-Eilean
(*Photo:* David Hayes)

Cluny, Chief of Clan
Macpherson, c. 1661
(National Galleries of
Scotland)

Mrs Anne Grant of
Laggan, by Jema Tanneck
(National Galleries of
Scotland)

The Laird of Grant's Piper. William Cumming, in full piper's panoply, in front of Castle Grant. By Richard Waitt, 1714. (National Museums of Scotland)

Malcolm Macpherson, 'Calum Piobair', of Cat Lodge, Cluny Macpherson's piper (died 1908)

The ferry boat at Insh (Kincraig)

The original ferry at Boat of Garten

(*Above*) Alvie Church, above Loch Alvie (*photo:* David Hayes)

(*Below*) Insh Church, above Loch Insh (*photo:* Madeline Russell)

The engraved east window in Insh Church (*photo:* Jane Richards)

The battle is very fully documented. A visit to the National Trust Information Centre on the battlefield will give the full picture of the tragic day. Most of the men leaving the field at Culloden were fleeing, disorderly. One contingent did leave with pipes playing and banners flying and made their way south to re-assemble with others at Ruthven Barracks, burnt and roofless though it was. Here, later, they received a message from the Prince – 'Disperse.' Each man's safety would be in his own hands. The dismay with which this was received remains for us in the emotion of the contemporary song, 'Will ye no' come back again?':

> Bonnie Charlie's noo awa'
> Safely o'er the friendly main,
> Mony a hairt would brak' in twa
> Should he no' come back again.

How many Badenoch men got safely back to their homes is not known. I have already written of the Rev William Gordon, the minister of Alvie, being hailed to Inverness for giving help to two survivors. All over Scotland there were men hiding in the heather, the Prince included, and Cumberland did not encourage mercy.

Prince Charles Edward's stay in this area in 'Cluny's Cage' brought danger here; there were more searches, more depredations, more tensions. It would have continued after the Prince had moved west, even after he had left the country. It is not recorded how much destruction there was here, but in Glen Moriston Lord Loudon, together with non-Jacobite Highland chiefs, 'went a-rummaging up and down the Glen, destroying all the ploughs, harrows, etc. pots, pans and all household furniture, not excepting the stone querns with which they grind their corn, breaking them in pieces and driving along with them such cattle as could be found...'

Balnespick, living at Dunachton, as I have said, was not 'out', but present on the lands he farmed, and 'the Good Laird', John Grant of Rothiemurchus, had died in 1743, thus never having to decide which side to support. His heir was a minor. Perhaps these circumstances helped to spare this area some of the worst of the repression and destruction, but for everyone it was a time of fear and oppression.

In the 'pacification' of the Highlands there were too many atrocities, too much destruction, too many fines and imprisonments; there was also the Disarming Act of 1746, when the following oath was administered, here as elsewhere; 'I, A.B., do swear as I shall answer God at the great Day of Judgement, I have not, nor shall have, in my possession any gun, sword, pistol, or other arm whatever, and never use tartan, plaid, or any part of the Highland garb; and if I do so, may I be cursed in my undertakings, family and property – may I never see my wife and children, father, mother, or relations – may I be killed in battle as a coward, and lie without Christian burial in a strange land, far from the graves of my forefathers and kindred; may all this come to me if I break my oath.'

In addition, the legal punishments were six months imprisonment for the first offence; for a second offence, seven years' transportation. This act was not repealed till 1782. but it must be admitted it was not always rigorously applied. We might pause to consider what alternative clothes a Highlander might have. There are portraits of this time showing the subjects wearing tartan clothes of every description, but of course the sitters of these portraits were men of influence not the poor folk of the land. (See Note 14, Tartan, p106.)

Another method used in the 'pacification' was the continued depopulation of the Highlands by drafting many men of fighting age into the regiments of the British Army, where they were used so effectively in Britain's wars abroad. They were, it is terrible to record, regarded as eminently 'expendable'. (See Note 15, Highland Regiments and the Militia, p108.)

Around 1750 the government ordered a secret survey of the Highlands, mainly with the object of discovering how many fighting men there were. It is made from the standpoint that the Highlands should be considered as a conquered but still hostile country. It was estimated that there were around 40 clans, of very different sizes and strengths. Camerons were noted as 'boasting of their firm adherence to the Protestant Religion' but though everyone was 'surprised at their resolution in the matter', they showed 'little regard for Religion in their Practice and are a wicked and Rebellious People.'

On Clan Chattan there is little detail. The writer reckons their area as 'Strathnairn, Strathdearn, Badenoch.' He notes that Macpherson and Macintosh both claim to be the 'Principal Branch'. Numbers of men able to bear arms are given: Macpherson, 400; Macintosh, 300; MacBeans, 100; MacGillivrays, 80; Shaws, 200; and 'also Davidsons, Smiths, McQueens, Nobles'. The Grants are not listed. The total count for the North of Scotland showed that 220,000 men were able to bear arms.

The survey also notes that no English was spoken by the 'common people'; (in Atholl, the German-speaking Hessian troops had to use Latin to make known their wants to the inn-keeper). Also that Enzie, Strathbogie, Strathdon and Glenlivet 'are inhabited by Papists and there is a college there for the training up of young men and strengthening the cause of Popery.' This implies that Presbyterianism was the pattern here, though some of the families in the south-west of Badenoch and around Loch Laggan remained Roman Catholic.

The writer of the survey makes suggestions for the future control of the Highlands: firstly that all Popish Priests should be forced to depart; secondly all Roman Catholics should be banned from owning land unless they allow their families to be instructed by Protestant ministers; thirdly new parishes should be formed (old medieval parishes were vast) and new churches built, as well as manses, and the stipends of ministers raised; and fourthly that schools should be built and schoolmasters appointed and paid.

It has already been pointed out that 'parliamentary' churches and manses were built here, but the 'schools in every parish', as with the similar plans of John Knox in the sixteenth century, did not get built. Badenoch, like other areas, had to wait another century for that, though Kingussie school continued its valuable existence and there was also a teacher at Ruthven township, and private schools were set up at times, including one at Alvie, later discontinued for lack of pupils.

After the '45 fighting as a way of life, ceased. Even cattle-reiving – previously considered a natural and necessary procedure – began to decline. In 1784 the Act of Restoration was passed, restoring property and titles to the exiled chiefs. The Macphersons held a great party to celebrate the lifting of the ban on Cluny, though most of the original 'caste' were dead or very elderly. Many had gone elsewhere, and the new regime of the chief as a landowner – often an absentee landlord receiving rents from 'tenants' – was slowly established. The clans, as units of control, had vanished.

History becomes an account of the way people lived.

8

WAYS OF LIFE

From run-rig to wire and wellies
1750–1900

Apart from the pain and misery deliberately inflicted on people and communities, many changes occurred in this period which brought real and lasting benefits to the Highlands. Generally many more records of all types are available to the researcher and much more information is easily accessible, about the ways of life in the Highlands. (See Note 16, Dr John MacKenzie, p110.) For example, Statistical Surveys, initiated and then masterminded and encouraged by Sir John Sinclair, were ordered by the Government to be made in each parish, and were made in 1798 and 1832, usually written by the minister of the parish. These surveys give a wealth of factual detail, and some opinions; they are the basis of modern history. Also after 1800 local newspaper archives can often provide detailed accounts of many events and people.

Housing was still often primitive and remained so in many areas through out this period, especially in the Highlands. The lay-out and style of the grander houses was another matter; here we can know of the Doune of Rothiemurchus, and Balavil and Dunachton, though all of them continually underwent alterations and improvements. (A Highland house of the previous century had been described by a government agent as usually having two doors to every room to aid the inhabitants' escape from enemies.) Although the black house at Kingussie Folk Museum is an Isles-type house, not of the Central Highlands, it gives some idea of what living conditions were like for many people. This exhibit is of course a dry and sanitised version of this kind of building. There are many folk still around who remember at least visiting an older relative living in this kind of house. The exhibition black house on Culloden Moor used to be visited by someone who has told me she 'never had a better scone than my aunt baked there.' However the new roads made it more possible to obtain and shift better building materials so that more modern house designs could be built. Many farm buildings and lodges of stone were built in this period. Pitmain House, part of the folk museum, shows an interesting wooden chimney piece, as well as furnishings spanning the years. The farm house of the 'Folk Park' outside Newtonmore has a particularly pleasing staircase. We should also notice the excellent cobble flooring on many of the old steadings. (The cobbled floor of Insh Church was only removed in 1912.)

In most farming tounships there were 'Tacksmen' (the chief tenant – and sometimes the representative of the laird), tenants, holding their land from the tacksman, and their sub-tenants. In addition there were cottars, having a small amount of land, possibly an acre, also servants employed by those who could afford to do so, owning nothing. The variations on this were enormous, and not to be confused with the crofting system of land tenure, widely though not invariably, established throughout the Highlands. Both systems were in operation around here. There were also part-time craftsmen, who might or might not also be ranked in any of the above capacities.

The farm work in 1750 was still run mainly on the run-rig pattern here, though changes were already occurring, and much land had already been converted, for one reason or another, into the field system. (See Note 17, The Run-rig System, p111.) These new fields allowed improvements which were not possible under the strip system of run-rig farming. One improvement, made in the late eighteenth century which was very effective and long-lasting, was the construction of field drains, many of which still function today. Some people – the gentry mostly – were able to improve their land by liming; the results of this also show up to this day, and many lime kilns are marked on the older maps and are visible structures still such as the one near Loch-an-Eilean. But many people could not afford to lime and preferred to grow potatoes. (See Note 18, Potatoes, p112.)

Here in these parishes, however, the likelihood of early and late frosts meant that hunger, and indeed famine, did not only occur in years of potato disease. The changes in farming practices are shown in Dr. Grant's study of Balnespick's farm account book, and of course continued after his day though it is not so easy to pinpoint them. It must be remembered that here the soil is poor – sand and gravel – with peat in some areas; in the Insh Marshes, the peat is forty feet deep. The farmed land is classed today as only grade III, if it is classed at all. The arable and grazing land lies at between 600 and 800 feet above sea level and has a very short growing season; frost can occur in any month. The Statistical Survey of 1798 says that the parishes of Alvie and Insh 'are as high as any in Scotland' above sea level. The Survey also remarks that 'the latitude gives a very short growing season.'

The main crops – oats, barley, rye and grass – could not be grown in sufficient quantity to feed the inhabitants and their beasts. Some flax was grown and worked, but because of the labour involved, brought little profit. A great deal of woollen 'white plaiding' was produced for sale, one of the main ways of obtaining money. Few dyes were available or used. Most of the land was sheep pasture; few cattle were kept. The Survey states there was 'a surprisingly short supply of timber' for the number of the inhabitants, but states that in some years there are records of wood being taken to Inverness and sold there, by people from Badenoch. (To imagine walking to Inverness with your wood-carrying pack pony, to gain a small amount of desperately needed money for the goods unobtainable here, reveals the hard life of the people living here.)

The generally sandy soil yielded quite good returns to the 'Scots' ploughshare, but the use of the 'new' English ploughshare often brought the disasters of erosion, especially after the frequent floods.

The 'Moray Floods' of 1829 stand as a well-remembered (and well-documented) record of very severe flooding. Donald Macpherson of Glen Feshie reported saving his wife and six children from being swept away, and saw the water 'less than 3 feet below the keystone of Feshie Bridge.' Unfortunately the records do not say exactly where his house was. John Grant, the saw-miller at Feshieside, saw his saw-mill under 4 feet of water at 8.00 am on August 4th in 1829. Both banks of the Feshie show the results of many floods and of the attempts to control them. The new dredging of 1993 is really only different because of the mechanical equipment now available. We have enough trouble with flooding today to understand the disastrous effect of flooding on subsistence farming, especially when we remember that everything had to be done by man-power.

The boundaries of the parishes are more difficult to establish today since they no longer used as units of government. The Statistical Survey gives the population in 1801 as 1,058, and estimated that the parish of Alvie carried about 1,104 black cattle; 510 horses; 7,000 sheep; 101 ploughs. (See Note 19, Population Figures, p112.) The parish registers unfortunately have not been well kept and so are unreliable, but the human stories kept in letters and diaries and memoirs bring us very close to the lives of the people they describe. Mrs Grant of Laggan (*Letters from the Mountains*) and Miss Eliza Grant of Rothiemurchus (*Memoirs of a Highland Lady*) have both written spirited accounts of the people and happenings at the end of the eighteenth century and the beginning of the nineteenth. (See Note 20, Mrs Grant of Laggan, p115.)

The gradual development of agriculture, the effect of the French Revolution and the Napoleonic Wars, the improved roads, the increase in literacy, all show in these vivid writings. One other factor of those times is brought home to us too, namely the high rate of infant mortality.

Although it might be unsafe to conclude that what went on in Laggan or Rothiemurchus also happened here, it is probable that the pattern of farm management was much the same. Many of the descriptions of people and scenes given by Miss Eliza Grant of Rothiemurchus and by Mrs Anne Grant of Laggan are very similar, and we can add to them knowledge gained from the earlier account books of Dunachton, interpreted by Dr I.F. Grant.

Mrs Grant, coming to Laggan as a bride in 1776, found it was expected of her to manage the Glebe farm. She was very glad to find her mother-in-law living in the cottage which was used as the manse, 'for I should have been lost and bewildered on my entrance to such a new scene, as the government of more than half a dozen servants, and the complicated economy of a farm, without such a monitress.' A good housewife, Anne Grant writes, must *not* be a good wife and mother; her duties as a manager come first. 'You Lowlanders have not an idea of the complicated nature of Highland farming, and the odd customs that prevail here.'

The manse was extended to be 'a comfortable cottage with four rooms, with closets and nurseries and a kitchen built out from it.' It lay at 'the foot of an arable hill beyond which was a lofty mountain' and beyond again extensive moors which provided all the fuel necessary. There was a garden, which provided small fruit; many trees had been planted. The honey-suckle on the porch of the cottage was luxuriant, and much delighted the occupants. Mrs Grant reckoned they held the farm 'at a very easy rent' (from the Duke of Gordon); it supported twelve milk cows and two hundred sheep, and had a good range of summer pasture. The farm supplied everything '*absolutely* necessary', including wool and flax.

The lady of the manse sketches out one July Monday in 1787, Monday being the day that all the dwellers in glens come down for the supplies. 'At four o'clock, Donald arrives with a horse loaded with butter, cheese, and milk. The former I must weigh instantly. He only asks an additional blanket for the children and a covering for himself; two milk tubs, a cog, and another spoon, because little Peter threw one of the set in the burn; two stones of meal, a quart of salt; two pounds of flax for the spinners, for the grass continues so good that they will stay a week longer. He brings the intelligence of the old sow being the joyful mother of a dozen of pigs, and requests something to feed her with. All this must be ready in an hour; before the conclusion of which comes Ronald from the high hills where our sheep and young horses are all summer, and only desires meal, salt, and women with shears, to clip the lambs, and tar to smear them. He informs me that the black mare has a foal, a very fine one, but she is very low, and I must instantly send one to bring her to the meadows.

73

Before he departs, the tenants who do us services come; they are going to stay two days in the oak wood, cutting timber for our new byre, and must have a competent provision of bread, cheese, and ale for the time they stay. Then I have Caro's breakfast to get, Janet's hank to reel, and a basket of clues to despatch to the weaver; K's lesson to hear, her sampler to rectify; and all must be over before eleven; while his reverence, calm and regardless of all this bustle, wonders what detains me, urging me out to walk...'

Mrs Grant thought that the custom of sending cattle and their keepers (mainly women and children) up the glens to use the summer pasture there, taking the pressure off the lower ground, was good for everyone, 'yet, as they must carry their beds, foods, and utensils, the housewife who furnishes and divides these matters, has enough to do when her shepherd is in one glen and her dairy-maid in another with her milk-cattle'. One of the great concerns of life at Laggan – or elsewhere where summer sheilings were used – was the settling of the time of the removals. Mrs Grant writes that she so much enjoys watching 'the procession' that she rises early for that purpose. 'The people look so glad and contented, for they rejoice at going up; but by the time the cattle have eat all the grass, and the time arrives when they dare no longer fish and shoot, they find their old home a better place, and return with as much alacrity as they went.' 1794 and 1795 were years of plenty hereabouts, though thin years further south, and Mrs Grant rejoices in the making of a fine haystack; the picture she draws is similar to ones which still took place into the 1920s. The relationships between all the workers, from the minister himself, down to the 'kitchen damsel', show a society in which 'the bond between the superior and inferior classes is a kindly one.' (This is written after a full and vivid description of a tenant's wedding.) One final example of the details in these letters, on December 25th, 1788 – 'the ink is frozen by the fire-place...'

Professor T.C. Smout in his excellent general *History of the Scottish people, 1590–1830*, writes of Scotland having crossed a watershed by 1830, after which date 'rapid change became the norm'. The industrial revolution and the agricultural revolution, the period of invention and the centralising of the population in the 'factory' areas, all had their effect on Badenoch. Although Professor Smout does not actually mention the district; he does however quote Eliza Grant, the 'Highland Lady', giving her glorious – and unflattering – account of worship in Rothiemurchus parish church.

It must also be remembered that in 1832 the men of Badenoch, as in the whole of Britain, received the vote. Prosperity did generally increase, though the effect of the boom in the herring industry, or, say, of Chadwick's sanitary reforms in the cities, were not necessarily felt here.

That many agricultural changes did occur here we have the evidence of the monument on Tor Alvie to the Duke of Gordon (erected after his death in 1836) who introduced farming improvements of many kinds all over his lands, including those in Badenoch. The old stone walls also are part of the evidence – cattle kept from arable land, land enclosed in fields for better manuring and management; the old run-rig system disappearing and now only sometimes visible in aerial photographs.

On the road up Glen Tromie the Killiehuntly fields are walled in the old manner but carry at short regular intervals a pierced or cupped stone upright, rising a foot or more above the coping stone of the wall, to carry the young tree trunks that would make the walls more stock-proof (much later they were used for water pipes). Walls also began to carry heavy iron stanchions set in the cornerstones and along the length of the walls to carry thick wires about 1–2 feet above the wall-top to make a dyke cattle-proof. Wire fences were introduced around 1860. The railways were fenced with posts and wire from the first.

Many walls we still see now were built in the second half of the nineteenth century to ensure that there was better control of the farm areas. It must be remembered that the Education Act of 1872 required all children to attend school. Children could no longer be regularly employed on the farms. The 'fine healthy system' of 'minding the coos' (as an old friend once put it) gradually came to an end.

The Rev John MacDonald who wrote the Statistical Survey

of 1832, wrote that the only historical event of past years was the notable confrontation of his predecessor, William Gordon, with the Duke of Cumberland in 1745! Writing of standards of education in his parish Dr John also wrote of the myths concerning fairies – that their coming to a district was preceded by whirlwinds... so the windy areas of Glen Feshie were 'obviously' much troubled by fairies. The minister explains that fairies had been 'expelled from Highland life' by 'the benevolent exertions of Principal Baird.' Alas, we are told no more. Eliza Grant, writing about 1830, concluded that fairies and the Shorter Catechism were inextricably confused in people's minds. The Statistical Survey of 1798 recorded that here few people could read, while Dr John reckoned that by the end of his ministry more than 35% could read. Principal Baird was, in fact, almost singlehandedly responsible for a very considerable increase in the general education as well as the Christian education of many thousands of poor children, especially in the Highlands. (See Note 21, Principal Baird, p118.)

The existence of 'school houses' up and down the glens shows the reality that this tremendous change brought to the way of life all over the district.

Ownership of land began to change more often. About 1800 the Duchess of Gordon bought and improved Kinrara. Her love of the place and all she did for it, made a considerable difference to Badenoch. Influential visitors (such as King Leopold of the Belgians, Queen Victoria's uncle, who visited here in 1821) brought insights into other ways of living as well as money for services and goods provided. The Duchess visited Kinrara regularly and happily between July and November each year until her death in 1812. Eliza Grant tells us much about the sparkling effect the Duchess's presence had on the district. Her innovations included the planting of the larch which was later so disliked by Lord Cockburn.

The Marquis of Huntly, the Duchess's son, never visited when he took over, and the 'absentee landlord blight' was felt very badly.

At Balavil (the Belleville) Sir James 'Ossian' Macpherson put that estate 'on the map'. The revived interest in Gaelic through out Scotland, and indeed, Europe, was one of the effects of his alleged discovery, about 1760, of the poetry of the bard Ossian. (See Note 22, Ossian, p119.) His daughter Juliet married Sir David Brewster, renowned as a scientist, and was influential for many years in the area. Macintosh lands included Balnespick, Dunachton, and South Kinrara, now known as Inshriach. Dalnavert, sometimes known as the Davochs of the Head, had been made over to The Macintosh as compensation for the illegal beheading of a Macintosh Chief while on a social call to the Earl of Huntly, an event of the distant past which now substantially increased the Macintosh lands in Alvie parish.

Dunachton Castle, formerly the main Macintosh stronghold here, had never been rebuilt after 1689, but the house and the steadings were constantly improved. The Duke of Gordon still owned Ruthven, still a small township, Pitmain, and the land on which Kingussie stood; in 1800 it had two inns. The Duke also owned the forests of Glen Feshie and Ben Alder; his land used three ploughs only, showing how little arable land there really was. The Macphersons held Invertromie, Phones and Invernahavon, Ettersill, Banchor and the mill lands of Kingussie. However during the late nineteenth century lands changed hands increasingly frequently; this was one of the results of the destruction of the clan system, with tenants of various standings paying rents with no service involved; also landowners more frequently lived elsewhere, not on their estates.

Right through the nineteenth century the poverty of the district is very constantly mentioned. The people were said to be averse to military service, though 'high-spirited and lively'. The Surveys speak of 'no Dissenters' in either parish – this of course was written before the Disruption of 1843. The church buildings were often in disrepair; Alvie Church, rebuilt in 1798, had to be re-built again in 1833, and was in a poor state again by 1849. Insh Church had its major repair (after 1792) in 1816, when the manse was built and the glebe lands set up. In 1810 the big manse beside Alvie Church was built; that year there were 100 communicants at Alvie. The population was reported to be 'hardy and long-lived'; deaths were recorded as being mainly from 'fevers and consumption' (tuberculosis). The population generally increased throughout the nineteenth century.

The rapid changes after 1830 were not as rapid as those of the twentieth century, though fast enough to alter the ways of life here very considerably. The most noticeable change – apart from the improvement of the roads and the coming of the rail-ways – would I think, have been the very considerable increase in the number of stone-built slate-roofed houses.

9
THE TWENTIETH CENTURY

Then and Now

A century is really longer than most life-times, and 'in living memory' – a rather elastic term – does not really take us from 1900 to 1993.

However we are impressed by our elders' memories and an event actually occurring before our own birthdate sometimes gets into our own memories, reinforced by what the 'grown-ups' have told us.

Professor Smout thought that 'rapid change' had become the norm after 1830, but the speed seems to have increased between 1900 and 1939, and even more between 1939 and 1994, when we have had such tremendous cultural, scientific, social, and even ethnic, changes.

In the first fifty years of the twentieth century two world wars devastated our population, accelerated scientific discoveries, and altered women's place in society. Women being part of the general work-force is not now a matter for discussion, and further efforts for women's rights have coloured the second half of the century. In country life, sharing of the work between women and men has long been accepted as normal, but in this second half of the century machines have so reduced the number of people needed for any agricultural work that the occupations of the population of this parish have altered entirely.

Today we can look at one man's lifetime – perhaps a long life – but a man born in 1900 can tell you of the roads of his childhood, and *we* can see the juggernauts on the 'new' A9. He can speak of his schooldays, ending when he was 12 or 14, (or even earlier) when Gaelic was still beaten out of children (as late as 1925), and we can see today's children with their computers and calculators...

Supplies now come here from every area. We expect to get milk all the year round. I have talked with a man born on a croft above Laggan, where the grazing was too poor to keep a cow through the winter, so she was sent 'down' to Laggan Bridge. 'And what did you drink?' I asked; 'Weel, there was a mannie who cam' round wi' a wee horsey-cart selling wee barrels of porter' – he gestured with his hands the size of the kegs... about 2 feet by 1 foot – 'We took that, and with our porridge too.'

The recollections of the older people whose young days were spent here makes us aware of some of the changes, in the kinds of meals, the kind of clothes, the ways of speech, the kind of jobs, and there are, of course, since the 1860s an increasing number of photographs, as well as newspaper archives. Some changes are distressing to some of us. I once drove an old lady, at her request, from Kincraig bridge past Loch Insh. She remembered it as an overgrown track, hiding the quiet and secret shores of the loch. The place was, to her eyes, desecrated by the happy, energetic and colourful activity of the Loch Insh WaterSports Centre. (We in 1993 newly mourn trees cut down in Aviemore Centre as well as much else happening in the path of progress.)

The pattern of roadways, tracks and paths has altered very considerably. The footbridge across the Spey at Spey Bank, whose last remnants disappeared in the floods of 1993, was an important factor in many people's lives; it certainly figures in postmen's recollections. There was – and is – no other footbridge until the Spey reaches Aviemore. The forestry plantations are one of the main alterations to the landscape. East of the Spey they hide the old trackways, such as 'the old road to Tombain', the scholars' road to the school at Lagganlia, and many others. Cock Street (I have not been able to find anyone who could explain the name), which has been partly kept open by forestry work, was a major track serving the houses above Dalnavert Farm, as well as the Dalnavert Flats where the militia once drilled. The new houses of the land now worked as a co-operative at Dalnavert, and the forestry houses on the B970 have replaced vanished smaller houses, whose stones are now grass-covered and almost invisible,

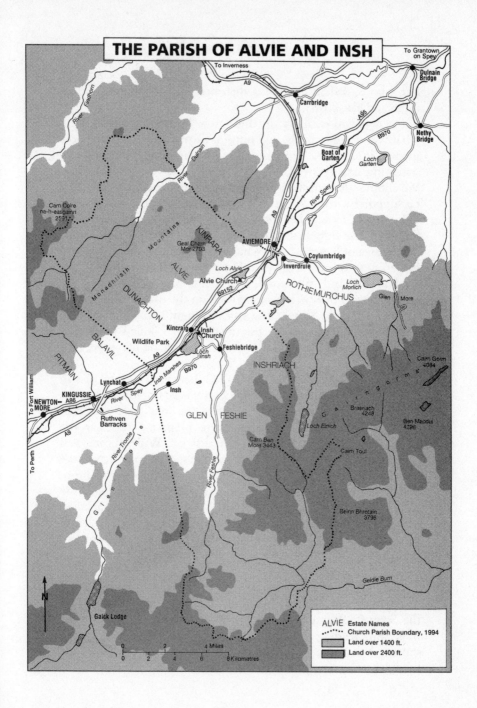

THE PARISH OF ALVIE AND INSH

To Grantown
on Spey

To Inverness

Dulnain
Bridge

Carrbridge

A9

A95

B970

Nethy
Bridge

River Dulnain

Boat of
Garten

Loch
Garten

River Spey

Carn Coire
na-h-easgainn
2531

KINRARA

Geal Charn
Mòr 2703

Mountains

AVIEMORE

Coylumbridge

ALVIE

Inverdruie

Loch Alvie

Loch
Morlich

Monadhliath

DUNACHTON

Alvie Church

ROTHIEMURCHUS

Glen   More

B9152

Kincraig

Insh
Church

Wildlife Park

Feshiebridge

BALAVIL

Loch
Insh

INSHRIACH

Cairn Gorm
4084

PITMAIN

A9

Insh Marshes

B970

Lynchat

Insh

Braeriach
4248

KINGUSSIE

River Spey

Ben Macdui
4296

NEWTON-
MORE

A86

To Fort William

Loch Einich

Ruthven
Barracks

GLEN   FESHIE

Cairn Ben
More 3443

Cairn Toul

River Tromie

To Perth

A9

River Feshie

Beinn Bhrotain
3795

Glen Tromie

Geldie Burn

N

Gaick Lodge

ALVIE	Estate Names
·········	Church Parish Boundary, 1994
▨	Land over 1400 ft.
▨	Land over 2400 ft.

0   2   4 Miles

0   2   4   6   8 Kilometres

81

but whose gardens are still sometimes visible outlined by daffodils and lilac bushes.

The standard of living in these new houses, compared with what was possible in the old houses, shows us how much more income is expected by those who live here now. It is repeatedly stated in past records that this is a 'poor', 'poverty-stricken' area. We should ask ourselves how can this higher standard of living be supported here? What money-making activities can provide the incomes to supplement those derived from agriculture and forestry? The bobbin-making mills – which were built in the station area of Kincraig, and where the Inshriach Alpine Nursery garden now is – used the plentiful birchwood, soft and suitable for bobbins, and gave employment resulting in several of the smaller houses in Kincraig being built on the road that continues past the Kincraig Stores. The mills brought that much needed extra income to the district, but the Great War 'killed' the industry, though the Kincraig mill survived, producing firewood, into the 1940s.

The Golf Club hut, and the Golf Course itself, on the flattish fields between Leault and the Suie Hotel have not long vanished. The new A9 and the re-alignment of the 'old' road cut clean across it. When the bulldozers were preparing to clear the ground for the new road, a specialist on Wade Roads was appointed to examine a series of trenches specially cut before the destructive work was done. He found, just below Dunachton, that the later nineteenth-century road, the coach road of the early 1800s, the Wade road of c1730, and a much older trackway, had all used the same narrow piece of land above Loch Insh and below the rocks of Dunachton and Suie. Thus we can appreciate that the lay-out of loch, river, and hill has put the same constraints on all road-builders.

Many details of life in the parish of Alvie and Insh are carried in the very valuable and excellent 'social' history compiled by the Scottish Women's Rural Institutes in 1967. It makes most interesting reading and leads to the hope that a similar study will shortly be made, showing the changes and recording our lifestyles today, thirty years later.

The talk of the older generation reveals a more closely knit community than we have nowadays. Families knew all about each other. A study of the electoral roll today (with the help of an old inhabitant) shows that many people moved into the district when the railways came. In the same way the roads brought new people as their construction needed new skills and more labour. Later the tourist industry brought many people of different skills to work here. (See Note 23, Employment, p121.)

Increased mobility, increased leisure, increased mechanisation, all mean that here, as elsewhere, the old ways of life have gone. Houses once used for farm workers are now – unless allowed to fall into ruin or disrepair – used as 'holiday' homes, or 'second' homes, or for the people working here but in jobs unrelated to farming. Some of this work comes from the need to supply short- or long-term visitors with food and services. New roads are built, are constantly upgraded and altered, and become busy with the distribution of 'consumer goods' as well as with cars and caravans. Long distance heavy traffic is now part of our lives too.

Obviously changes in housing create one of the most visible alterations in the landscape. Planners make rules about 'traditional' styles but many varied styles are built and often the 'Macleod Bungalow' seems to predominate. Villages and hamlets increase all the time. The increase in the number of houses and in the varied styles is seen if you walk along the B970 through Insh village, and then round the new loop road past the new houses. The use of timber, and of tiles instead of slates (few slates are quarried in Scotland today making slate roofs expensive), are two of the main features to be seen in modern houses.

House prices are high, usually above the reach of the first-time buyer. (See Note 19, Population Figures, p112.) A survey of the shops in Aviemore reveals that its main business is tourism whereas Kingussie and Newtonmore cater also for 'locals'. In Kincraig we still have our invaluable Kincraig Stores, with its Post Office, which is a great service to us all, without which we would be much less a village, much less a community. But supplies come from quite a distance; bread from Aberlour – and

Glasgow – as well as Kingussie; fruit and vegetables are now trucked in in greater quantities, available now as they were not fifty or even fifteen years ago. Milk we expect to be able to have fresh each day, often from a dairy firm at Elgin, rather than from local cows. (See Note 24, The Snowstorm of 1976, p122.)

The increased need for electricity, water, sewerage – all effect the landscape. Today's children accept the existence of and need for powerline pylons marching over the hills, which was opposed by earlier generations (telephone lines are now more frequently buried); the rivers serving hydro-electric schemes have often shrunk – the effect on the Garry is noticeable as we drive over Drumochter. We have no piped North Sea gas here, so gas fuel tanks are part of the village scene. The water mains now serve so very many more houses; the supply from Glen Einich is now widely used and far fewer homes rely on 'own water supply'. Septic tanks however still serve many people, and mains drainage is severely limited; indeed it is one of the main causes limiting the increase of housing developments.

The estates of Balavil, Dunachton, Alvie, Glen Feshie, Kinrara and Rothiemurchus are still very much in existence and are very involved in the tourist trade. Apart from leasing houses, cottages and chalets, on short term lets, the 'cream of the business' as one land-owner put it, is in the leasing of the stalking, shooting and fishing rights. Rothiemurchus, which lies outwith our parish, remains in the Grant family, is coping with tourism in many imaginative ways and is a big employer of labour. It has its own Visitor Centre, Ranger service, and much else as well as a most informative 32 page guidebook. Rothiemurchus attracts more than 300,000 visitors a year. It is a notable employer of local labour as well as 'foreigners'.

Alvie Estate has certainly taken up the challenge of 'diversification'. It has a flourishing sawmill, controlled clay-pigeon shooting, a brown trout-stocked fishing loch, as well as houses and flats for holiday lets and longer term tenancies. The Dalraddy Caravan Park has a vigorous life of its own as well. However it is almost impossible to make a worthwhile profit on this marginal land however well managed. Far fewer people are employed, motorised transport making it possible for one man to be in many places in one day, whether he is dealing with stock, timber, supplies or harvesting. Alvie is being managed to get the best returns from its assets, but is not going to be able to make big profits on the traditional use of the land in farming and forestry. The sporting rights and activities, together with high quality accommodation, bring good business to the area, with a considerable spin-off to local employment, craft shops, services, and all trades. All the farm and forestry business is managed by computer programmes expertly worked out and increasing enormously the efficiency of the estate. Selling computer expertise and management on a national and international scale is already the activity which earns the greatest income here, far outstripping the income possible from the land. This may well be a future pattern for wealth-making in this area.

Since far fewer people make a living from the land today, tourism has become the major source of income. Since the skiing industry began to develop in the 1960s the 'double tourist season' of summer and winter visitors has resulted in a tremendous expansion, so that five or so 'poor' winters, when skiing was very limited (or non-existent) has been very damaging to the local economy. Trade of all kinds suffered; the national recession and the drop in overseas visitors mean that now too much tourist accommodation is chasing too few visitors.

I think it is also true to say that the picture which we try to give to tourists of the 'Highland Life', is no longer natural. The old customs, styles of dress and entertainment are artificially enacted for the tourists' benefit. The many incomers have absorbed some of the flavour of life in this area, old customs, habits and styles are still remembered by a few. The independence of mind, the acceptance of hard work, devotion to the land around us, to our homes, these are still present, but the twentieth-century pressures and comforts do affect us all. Do we really want to return to the cold, simple, frugal lifestyle of 1900? We like our food supplies, our plumbing, our water supplies; our double-glazing, our own cars, computers and electric blankets... This beautiful strath yields tremendous rewards to those who visit it for whatever purpose.

'Outdoor Education' is a new industry which is now well catered for here. Loch Insh Watersports is an excellent example of this. Lothian Region owns and runs Lagganlia Centre for Outdoor Education above Feshie Bridge; the RAF have a hostel close by, using other training establishments for their clients; there is a small hostel up Glen Feshie which is ideal for hill-walkers, cross-country skiers, naturalists of any kind. The Badenoch Christian Centre, in Kincraig itself, caters for groups of every kind who want to enjoy what this parish has in abundance – the 'outdoors'. The Centre was purpose-built so that the Church of Scotland could offer to everybody who chooses to come, a Christian base here, where serious talk and thought, worship and prayer (and much laughter) can take place beside the physical pleasures and skills of walking, climbing, skiing, canoeing, wind-surfing, which can be so well enjoyed here.

Over the years agricultural policies have altered the use and appearance of the land. We can still notice land that had been worked in previous generations, often shown by being visibly greener, because it was once limed, as well as by old walls. The old maps show 'sheep fold' marked on many places, usually stone built rectangles. Nowadays sheep are shifted by sheep float; cattle are shifted by cattle trucks; all needing expensive tracks and roads. Wire fences have replaced walls almost everywhere; these are now sometimes deer fences, put up to keep deer out of plantations, on the moors, or in deer farms. There is a deer farm at Rothiemurchus. We also have trout farms at Rothiemurchus (rainbow) and Alvie (brown trout) with fishing in stocked lochs. These cater for a trade that did not previously exist.

The biggest landscape changes are perhaps due to forestry. Trees are a crop which can use, and make profitable, land on which little else would thrive; but the blanket forestry is still a blight from which Badenoch might be glad to be delivered. Forestry policies and practices change the landscape, needing tracks and roadways which get ever bigger as the equipment does.

More changes will come. Badenoch is now 'on the map'. No

longer hard to reach, yet perhaps the quality of life here is still what brings people to this beautiful and blessed place, whatever way their living is earned. It is a place that becomes beloved by its people. The Rev Thomas Sinton, collecting ancient poetry and songs hereabouts, heard – once only – a beautiful, soft, nostalgic air, the words of which held a deep love of these glens:

> 'Glen Feshie of the storm blasts
> Within your shelter I would be
> Where I would find the blaeberry
> The cloud of black berries,
> Round nuts on the hazel,
> And red fish in the linns.'

The people have changed. Ways of life have vastly changed. In spite of the new roads, the hills, the lochs, the skies remain.

Perhaps I should end by quoting what the Rev A.D. MacRae wrote when he updated his account of this united parish in 1954:

> 'There is possible here a way of life – inspired and drawing its strength from the teachings of the Bible which since earliest times has been continuously preached here.
>
> 'The people of this parish enjoy a measure of prosperity, unknown to their forefathers. They look ahead with quiet trust, believing that "the best is yet to be."
>
> 'The mountains, glens, lochs and rivers draw to their hearts the travellers, and the seekers after quiet and beauty, while upon those who sojourn here in their midst, they bestow their benediction of a tranquil outlook, a peace which comes from the hills – "even from the Lord who hath made Heaven and earth."'

Notes

Note 1. Queen Victoria's Highland Expeditions

The diaries of Queen Victoria reveal a delightful picture of this part of the world, coloured, of course by the Queen's character and views. They are well worth reading. Having settled at Balmoral the Queen made many expeditions across the hills from Braemar. On September 4th 1860, the Queen and Prince Albert with Lady Churchill and Lord Grey, and a support team of pony men and John Brown, drove from Balmoral past the Linn of Dee to where the Geldie joins the Dee. There they mounted ponies and rode or walked – 'the ground was so soft and boggy in places that we had to get off and walk several times' – up the Geldie and then down the Feshie – 'a fine rapid river'.

Fording the Eidart with some difficulty the party made their way down the Feshie to the levels where 'the native fir trees were particularly fine; we were quite enchanted with the beauty of the view.' Continuing down to Loch Insh, the royal party crossed the Spey by the ferry, the Boat of Insh, to meet a coach previously ordered. The ferry was 'a very rude affair, like a boat or coble, but we could only stand in it; it was moved by two long oars plied by the ferry man and Brown, and at the other end by a long sort of beam which Grant [a pony man] took in hand.' The ponies were sent back the next day, by the way they had come, and the royal party drove on to Grantown-on-Spey, where they spent the night incognito. Queen Victoria writes: 'dined well on soup, hodge-podge, mutton-broth with vegetables, fowl in white sauce, good roast lamb, very good potatoes… ending with a good tart of cranberries.' The next day, driving, riding and walking, they returned to Balmoral by way of Tomintoul, Glen Avon and

Inchrory – a strenuous two days.

The second time the Queen records a visit to these parts is on October 8th 1861 when another ride over the Geldie and Feshie route again enchanted the Queen. This time, at Loch Insh they turned south, 'along a high road, past the ruined castle at Ruthven and over a long wooden bridge to an inn at Kingussie – a very straggling place with very few cottages.' They then went 'on and on… it became very cold and windy with occasional rain.' 'We reached the inn at Dalwhinnie, which stands by itself away from the village – 29 miles from where we left the ponies.' The day's total mileage was 60 miles. The rooms were satisfactory but not the food. 'Unfortunately there was only tea and two starved Highland chickens, without any potatoes! NO pudding and no fun!'

The next day they went on to Blair Castle, then up the Tilt and down the Dee, and so back to Balmoral – another total of 60 miles riding and driving.

Note 2. Guide Books

Much fascinating detail can be found in the guide books of the 1890s. Having shown how a destination – say Kingussie – might be reached, the Guide Book describes many walks, and some drives (by pony cart), and the writers go out of their way to call this area 'remarkably picturesque and beautiful'. Badenoch is described as 'an immense tract of highland territory' and another writer comments that 'it is only by plunging into the very heart of the East Grampians that we can fairly appreciate their vast proportions.' In this age of the car, most distances have shrunk, and we can certainly drive further 'into' the hills, so we need to be reminded of the true size of the Grampians. Black's 1892 *Guide to Scotland* says 'great numbers of sheep from the north are put on the train at Dalwhinnie for the south', but Murray's *Handbook for Travellers* of 1898 calls Dalwhinnie 'a desolate and solitary spot', but writes approvingly of Dalnaspidal Station. We are apt to ignore the presence of Dalnaspidal and even Dalwhinnie today. This guide also tells us to pronounce Kingussie (giving the Gaelic meaning, 'end of the pinewood') as KINYEWSSIE, and speaks of the good turf apparent as the strath widens after the barren hills of Drumochter.

Baedeker's 1897 *Guide* shows how to travel by rail and boat. This makes evident the multiplicity of railway companies; the Highland Line, from Perth to Inverness direct (described as one of the most beautiful lines in three kingdoms), at that date only went as far as Carrbridge so that the Speyside line from Aviemore via Forres had to be used to reach Inverness.

Walking routes described include Braemar to Insh (which had an inn), and Braemar to Aviemore (which had a hotel) via the Larig Ghru – 33 miles – as well as the Gaick and Minigaig passes and the Glen Feshie–Geldie route to Braemar. The walks from Kingussie 'beyond the new golf course' are also described. These guide books are based on people's ability and willingness to walk, as modern guide books are not, though there are, of course, books such as *Low level Walks in Speyside*.

Note 3. The Railways

In the 1860s, railway companies were being formed all over Britain, and the profits to be won meant that competition was keen between the different routes planned. The Highland Railway Company, formed in 1865 to construct a railway from Inverness to Wick and from Inverness to Perth, had the first sod cut by the Countess of Seafield. The Company faced fierce opposition from the company building the Perth–Aberdeen–Nairn line.

The direct route, over Drumochter, had been thrown out as early as 1846, but engineering methods were developing all the time, and the skills and persistence of the engineer Joseph Mitchell conquered not only the difficulties at Killiecrankie, the wide Tay at Dalguise, and the spate problems of the river Tilt, but also the difficulties of satisfying the Duke of Atholl about the crossing of the river Garry above Calvine.

Snow blocks were – and are – prevented to a large degree by the ingenious placing of the track, well-used snow-ploughs, and much hard work. The gradients at Struan and Dalnacardoch of 1:65 and 1:70 were the steepest yet built. It must also be noted that men on Drumochter could sometimes only work for four hours a day because of the very severe frosts. The viaducts at Slochd, Tomatin, and even more impressive perhaps, the Strath–Nairn viaduct speak for themselves of skills, dedication, and a change in the life of those served by this railway. It was always thought of as being built for the Highlanders themselves, especially the Invernessians, not for visitors. One guide book of the time suggests that the roads would fall into total disrepair now that the railways had come.

Building the railway was a costly venture, and a minor point of punctuality had to be faced too. There are 29 stations between Perth and Inverness, and 30 between Inverness and Wick. Half a minute's extra chat at each station, harmless though it seemed, multiplied to an unacceptable half hour. Despite this difficulty to Highland employees, Badenoch was entering the greater world. The O.S. Maps were produced in conjunction with the railway engineers.

Those printed after the arrival of the railways show details of the housing and roads. There are about ten croft houses and strips of croft land at Lynchat; there are several footbridges across canals on the marshes. There are about eleven croft houses and strips at Insh; Soillerie is also marked, the Mission Hall (now the church there). None of the large villas of Kincraig appear in the first edition of the map. The ferry-man's house at Boat of Insh is marked, and the inn that stood behind it. The Church is marked 'Quoad Sacra' meaning that it was not at that time the centre of a civil parish. The Manse, now Insh House Guest House, was a Telford building, then not fifty years old. The second edition of this map shows Insh Church as 'on the site of 'St Ewan's Chapel' but this ascription should probably be 'St Eunan's Chapel'. A study of successive editions of the maps is rewarding, showing many changes – buildings appearing and buildings vanishing. Perhaps one of the oldest continuously used sites is Baldow Smithy.

By 1874 the bridge across the Spey has been built; the large villas are mapped and the bobbin makers houses; there is a post office. Kincraig has come into being – all because of the coming of the railway and the building of the station at Kincraig.

Note 4. The Clava Cairns

This group of three cairns (O.S. map reference NH754 440) has been excavated, 'stabilised' and dated as far as is possible, though the lack of evidence, mainly due to robbing, leaves us with a vague 'late Stone Age' ascription, between 2000 and 1500 BC. They lie beside the river Nairn at Balnuaran and there are five more within a mile. The type name 'Clava' has been given to these and to twenty-seven others along the Ness, Enrick, Nairn and Spey rivers. There are none on the Findhorn.

These are chambered cairns, corbelled, using roughcut stones; used for burials and also possibly for worship. The remarkable features are that they have large cobbled platform areas around the cairn with a ring of monoliths or standing stones. These features are not found elsewhere. The entry passage is on the south-west, thus possibly connecting then with a ceremony based on the winter solstice. They were built before the recumbent stone circles of the north-east of Scotland, and some archaeologists have considered a possible Mediterranean influence.

A feature which remains inexplicable is the presence of several stones marked with the mysterious cup-and-ring carvings. It is possible that these stones were already on a sacred site when the cairns were built.

The nineteenth-century excavators speak of bones and 'grave goods' within the cairns, but these are now lost so that carbon dating is not possible on them.

Further references: James Fraser, *Proceedings of the Society of Antiquaries of Scotland*, 1883–4.

Professor Stuart Piggot, P.S.A.S.

Note 5. The Pictish Symbol Stone

From *Early Christian Monuments of Scotland*, J. Romilly Allen. 1903. (p.100.)

Dunachton

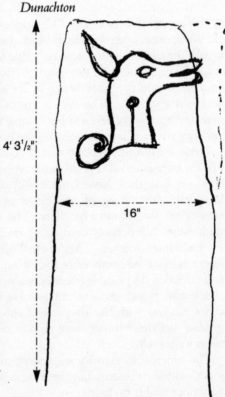

This place is situated in the valley of the Spey immediately to the west of Loch Insh, and a mile and a half S.W. of Boat of Insh Railway Station. (Ordnance Survey Map, 74.)

The symbol stone was found in 1870 as a lintel over a doorway in an old steading at Dunachton, the stones of which were used in building Dunachton Lodge, and was preserved and moved to its present position by Mr C. Fraser Mackintosh of Lochardil, then commissioner for the Mackintosh of Mackintosh, proprietor of Dunachton. It has been

4' 3½"

16"

erected on a sandstone base on the terrace at the south corner of the garden about a hundred yards from the front door of the lodge. Unfortunately a portion of the right upper corner of the stone, including part of the upper lip of the figure, has been broken away.

It is a slab of diorite stone, 4 ft. 3½ inches high, by 16 inches wide, by 4½ inches thick; sculptured with incised lines on one face.

Front: – Close to the top of the stone the beast's head symbol, ornamented on the neck with a vertical line terminating in a small round cup, and at the lower left hand corner with a curved line with a similar termination.

It is classified as a Class I, Early Incised stone.

I do not think it is a Christian Monument.

Note 6. Sites of archeological interest in Badenoch and Strathspey

A fuller list may be obtained from the Highland Regional Council, but here is a list of the main sites for this area, with a few more distant ones which add to our understanding of the evidence of the past around us.

Prehistoric ritual and funerary

NH 897 134	Aviemore, chambered cairn and stone circle.
NH 844 085	Easter Delfour, chambered cairn and stone circle.
NH 907 155	Loch na Carraigean, chambered cairn and stone circle 3,200m north of Aviemore.
NH 863 989	Loch Alvie ring cairn.
NH 909 167	Avielochain Chambered cairn. (Clava Type.)
NH 912 174	Cranog in Loch Vaa.

Prehistoric, domestic and defensive

NH 905 172	Avielochain, Tor Beag fort.
NN 582 929	Dun-da-lamh fort.
NH 776 019	Lynchat, souterrain, 550m. WNW of Kingussie.

Carved stones

| NH 820 046 | Dunachton Lodge, symbol stone. |
| NJ 026 620 | Inverallan Churchyard, symbol stone. |

Ecclesiastical

NH 938 155	Kincardine church.
NH 822 046	St Drostan's Chapel, within walled burial ground.
NN 705 989	St Bridget's Chapel, (site of) and burial ground.
NN 536 896	St Kenneth's Church (remains).

Secular

NJ 006 219	Castle Roy, Nethy Bridge.
NN 528 943	Garva Barracks, Garvamore.
NN 521 947	Garva Bridge, over River Spey.
NN 764 997	Ruthven Barracks, Kingussie.
NH 898 079	Loch-an-Eilein Castle.
NJ 039 263	Old Spey Bridge, Grantown-on-Spey.

Permission should be obtained from the landowner before visiting any of these sites.

Note 7. Druids

It is hard to be factual about the Druids, as medieval writers have obscured the reports of Julius Caesar with myths; worse, nine-teenth-century writers promulgated so many other myths about the Druids that they more or less 're-created' them. Druids flour-ished roughly between 200 BC and 500 AD in western and northern Europe, including Britain. How far north they were established is debatable. Historians rely for first-hand accounts on Julius Caesar's encounters with Druids during his conquest of Gaul and his campaigns in Britain which led to the Roman conquest of England and southern parts of Scotland (c70 BC).

The Druids were reputed to have tremendous powers and were certainly very much feared. The word 'druid' may stem from an ancient Erse word meaning 'wise' or 'very knowing'.

Caesar reckoned that 'all men of any rank or dignity in Gaul' were connected in some way with the Druids; that they were in effect 'the learned and priestly class'. It would be the Druids who expounded and guarded the laws, while always veiling their procedures with deepest secrecy.

Caesar reports that they had power to inflict severe penalties for disobedience, the severest, most dreaded, being the total excommunication from society. Druids were exempt from taxes and from military service, thus making entry to their ranks very attractive. They often seemed to be more powerful than kings or chiefs. The leader was elected by the members; no office was hereditary; novices had prolonged and intensive training. All instructions were orally transmitted; perhaps this, with the vows of secrecy, accounts for our lack of accurate knowledge.

The Roman historian, Cicero, reports that the Druids taught belief in an immortal soul which could be transferred (as Pythagoras taught) to other bodies, not necessarily human, irrespective of time and space.

They allegedly studied astrology, and did study astronomy; they were thought to use the ancient stone circles and standing stones, erected perhaps 2,000 years before their time, to enhance their predictions and rulings. Cicero thought that Druids studied geography and the physical sciences to acquire knowledge similar to that of the Greeks and Egyptians.

Sacrifices – both human and animal – were part of the cult, and the secrecy, indeed mystery, as well as their knowledge, gave the Druids much power. It is certain they were very much feared. Oak groves in remote forests, tidal islands, and strange rock formations, were used as power bases; mistletoe, that strange parasite of oaks, was connected with their rites.

Druids were banned in the Roman Empire, by Caesar Augustus and again by Tiberius.

Their power seems to have been overcome, not without difficulty, by the rise of Christianity.

Note 8. List of Ministers

List of Ministers of the parish of Alvie

1567–1569	Alexander Clark
1570–1579	John Glass
1580–1585	William MacIntosh
1586	SOVERAINE Macphail
1595–1597	Robert Leslie
1599–1601	Roderick Sutherland
1614–1618	William Fraser
1619–1626	James Lyle
1632–1642	Roderick MacLeod
1642–	Alexander Clark
1652–	James Watson
1662–	James Dick
1662–1708	Thomas Macpherson
1711–1721	Alexander Fraser
1728–1738	Lewis Chapman
1710–1787	William Gordon
1788–1805	John Gordon
1806–1854	John MacDonald
1854–1870	Donald Macdonald
1880–1913	James Anderson
1914–1932	Dugald Maclean

United with the parish of Insh

1933–1948	Archibald F. Shaw
1949–1954	Alexander MacRae

1954–1960	William Campbell
1960–1978	Alexander Hutchison
1978–	John R. Lyall

Note 9. Alvie Church

Alvie Church, by one tradition, was dedicated to St Ailbhe, a saint of the 'Culdees' (holy men of the period between the early Celtic Church of the monks, and the medieval church). By tradition St. Ailbhe founded a cell by Loch Alvie. A great deal of alteration has taken place in the present building; the altar was probably removed at the time of the Reformation, and there were galleries with the pews under them at the short walls, with the pulpit in the centre of the north-west wall, and the main pews running the long length of the church. The main rebuilding of the Church was in the 1790s, as part of the Government policy to pacify the Highlands, but the building needed constant repair. In 1850 it was decided to replace the cobbled floor with a wooden one; in lifting the cobbles the skeletons of 150 men were discovered. No one thought to investigate further, or to date the weapons found with them. The bones and weapons were simply re-buried in the graveyard. The stone above them is inscribed:

> 'Their bones are dust.
> Their good swords rust,
> Their souls are with the Lord, I trust.'

Thus we can only surmise that this is further evidence of the 'Age of Forays', evidence of a particularly savage clan battle. There are legends of apparitions, of ghostly keenings, but no real tradition of so many men having lost their lives at one time around Loch Alvie.

Alvie Church was renovated in 1952, directed by the architect Sir Basil Spence. Mrs Williamson of Alvie and Lord Bilsdon of

Kinrara provided the driving force behind the alterations which give us the lovely church we have now. The church has been refurbished again in August 1994 and we rejoice in the added light and space. If one drives south on the old A9 Alvie Church can be seen across the stretch of Loch Alvie, still witnessing to the Christian faith practiced here.

Note 10. Insh Church

I think we have to assume that all the records of Insh made prior to 1838 were lost, either by fire (as they were in Kingussie Church in 1725, and again in 1925), or just 'lost'.

We can record that Mr Lewis MacPherson was ordained and inducted into the Pastoral Charge of Insh on March 15th 1837. His elders are listed as:

James MacPherson	1811
Alex MacLean	1813
Angus MacBain	1829
Wm Grant	1834

Further entries in that Session Book are mainly concerned with the monies for the poor, the few payments to the Church Officers, and the date of Communions with the numbers attending.

In 1891 the Rev David Munro left for Edinburgh for an eye operation. He then retired, having been minister of this parish for 48 years.

Bad weather frequently prevented services being held. In 1929, following the well-established custom, Fast Day Services, when communion tokens were issued, were still held on the Thursday preceding the two Communion Sundays, but I have not found a record of when these were discontinued. Preparation Services followed on Saturday. In many areas a Thanksgiving Service took place on Monday, often followed by a closing dinner for all visiting ministers, usually a convivial and hearty meal.

In 1929, 20 members at Communion was held to be 'SATIS-FACTORY'. There are many blanks in this session book and it is only half-used. In 1921 it is recorded that the minister was absent 'for the last six months' on military service in Russia. Later a vacancy was declared in 1929 and this was finally resolved by the union with the parish of Alvie in 1933 under the Rev Archibald Shaw.

It is believed that the church was built on the site of a very early Christian teaching centre. The church building was renovated in the 1790s, as part of the Government scheme to 'exterminate Popery'. Afterwards the outside walls were reasonably sound but constant repairs were necessary. In 1861 the Session of the Parish of Insh wrote to Sir George Macpherson-Grant, on the occasion of his coming of age, complaining of the 'deplorable condition' of Insh Church; that it was a 'dark, unsightly, uncomfortable, and unwholesome place of worship.' Moreover, they complained, it was four miles from their crofts, in Insh village, where ' clearances' had established some ten crofts for those folk removed from Glen Feshie. This letter was signed by Shaw of Tolvah and 38 others. The answer was that Sir George would be 'glad to act'. There is no exact record of what was done, though the deeds for the building of the Manse (now Insh House Guest House) cast some light on the matter.

In 1869 the parish of Insh was 'disjoined' from Kingussie as a 'Quoad sacra' parish and land was transferred later.

There is then a considerable gap in the session records.

There were galleries at both the east and west ends of the church. The pulpit was in the middle of the long wall (on the loch side), and the bell was chained on the windowsill beside it. Also, set into that window sill was the huge granite stone used as a font. Opposite the pulpit was the entrance to the church. By the 1880s the galleries had been removed, the pulpit placed in front of the pews which had been re-aligned to face east (actually, north east). The old door had been built up, and a large black stove placed in the alcove; a new entrance and vestry had been formed at the south-west end of the church. The cobbled floor was removed about 1910–12.

Plans resulting in the most recent renovations to the church were initiated in 1962/3. The Rev Alex Hutchison, together with both Mrs Williamson of Alvie, and Lord Bilsdon of Kinrara, were instrumental in this. The Carey family, owners of the villa Morven in Kincraig, also wanted to set up a memorial to their uncle, F.P. Milligan, who had a 90-year lease of Farr. Their first suggestion was to move the ancient granite font to the front of the church, but this proved impracticable. Finally the old stone was set in the entry to the church, where it still is. It was still sometimes used as a font, though often a crystal bowl was used. The Careys decided on the elegant wooden font we use today, the eight panels being carved with symbols, designed by the Rev A. Hutchison, showing the stages through which the church has passed.

The architect for this renovation was Schönberg Scott, who also designed the wrought-iron doves supporting the ancient bronze bell, symbolising the flame of the Holy Spirit with the doves of St Columba. Mr Hutchison reports that a 'little man from Nethy Bridge' came to offer money so that from door or window the world outside could be seen during worship. This was done. There was much opposition to the clear glass, though it was discovered that the coloured glass (mauve, pink and mustard lozenges) had been in the windows for less than fifty years. The engraved cross in the north-east window is from the design of St John's Cross which stands outside the west door of Iona Abbey. The late Helen Turner, of the Edinburgh College of Art, designed and executed this; it is sandblasted on the panes. (The seven panes were actually only inserted in the window on the Saturday before the dedication.)

The dedication service took place on Sunday May 31st 1964, and was conducted by the Rev George Macleod, leader of the Iona Community, Bishop Carey, and the Rev Alex Hutchison.

For a detailed study of the influence of the Church throughout Scotland there is a marvellous and comprehensive book, with a wealth of detail, *Candie for the Foundling* by Anne Gordon. It gives a lively, if sometimes unflattering picture of the Kirk through the centuries since the Reformation. I have not found any detail referring to these parishes, nor, I think, to anywhere in this Presbytery.

Note 11. The Piper's Memorial

There is a small Celtic cross at Kincraig, opposite the War Memorial on the old A9 which is inscribed as follows:

> This cross has been
> erected in memory of
> Piper Peter Stewart
> and his brave comrades
> who for Queen and country
> fell in the battle of Atbara
> on the Nile on April VIII.
>
> MDCCCXCVIII

Atbara is the most southerly major tributary of the Nile. At the confluence of the river Atbara and the Nile, General Sir H. Kitchener defeated the Mahdi's forces very decisively, thus paving the way for the total destruction of the Mahdi's power at the battle of Omdurman in 1899.

General Wauchope was in command of a force comprising 'the Lincolns, the Seaforths and the Camerons.' Their casualties were 'light'; the Zareiba was taken with at least 3,000 'Arabs' killed. There were of course 'native' forces under Kitchener's command.

The following extract comes from the Records of The Cameron Highlanders. Vol. I, concerning the battle of Atbara.

'Some of the fiercest fighting took place at a circular stockade which was built inside the "dem" some 30 yards from the Zariba. It was held by about 1,000 of Mahmoud's chosen followers, who fought with desperate courage. From this stockade a heavy and incessant fire was poured on the assailants, the chief sufferers being the Cameron Highlanders, the Lincolnshire regiment, and the 11th Sudanese. Indeed, one company of the latter Battalion was almost annihilated in an attempt to gain an entrance. It was here that Piper Stewart of the Camerons met his death. He had reached some rising ground, where, undaunted by bullets whizzing past him, he continued to play "The March of the Cameron Men" until he was struck down. His body was found afterwards to have been pierced by no less than seven bullets.'

There is a painting in the Regimental Mess of the battle of Atbara with the Seaforths and the Camerons storming the Zareba.

Peter Stewart is officially known to the Camerons as Piper James Stewart, but no doubt his family knew him as Peter. It is thought that this Stewart family lived on Dunachton, at the cottage – now ruined – above Loch Insh, across from the church.

I have been told that this is the only known monument to a single piper, though tales of their heroism and of the power of the pipes are told of many campaigns, from the relief of Lucknow to El Alamein, to name only two.

Note 12. Chan Chattan

The Clan Chattan Association includes:

Clan Mackintosh

Adamson	Esson	MacClerich	MacNiven
Ayson	Glen	MacChlery	MacRitchie
Aysons of N.Z.	Glennie	McConchy	Niven
Clark	Gollan	Macglashan	Noble
Clarke	Heggie	MacHardie	Ritchie
Clarkson	Hardie	Machardy	Tarrill
Clerk	Hardy	Machay	Tosh
Crerar	MacAndrew	Mackeggie	Toshach
Dallas	MacAy	McKillican	
Elder	MacCardney	MacLerie	

Clan Macpherson

Cattanach	Gillespie	MacCurrach	MacMurdoch

Clark	Gillies	MacGowan	MacMurrich
Clarke	Gow	MacKeith	MacVurrich
Clarkson	Keith	MacLeish	Murdoch
Clerk	Lees	MacLerie	Murdoson
Currie	MacChlerich	MacLise	
Fersen	MacChiery	MacMurdo	

Clan Shaw

Ayson (N.Z.)	Adamson	Esson	MacAy
MacHay	Shiach	Sheach	Sheath
Seith	Seth	Skaith	Scaith
Shay			

Clan Macbean

Bain	McBain	McBeath	Macilvian
Bean	MacBean	MacBeth	MacVean

Clan Farquharson

Coutts	Grevsach	MacCardney	MacKerracher
Farquhar	Hardie	MacEaracher	Mackinlay
Findlay	Hardy	MacFarquhar	Reach
Findlayson	Leys	MacGruaig	Riach
Finlay	Lyon	MacHardie	
Finlayson	MacCaig	MacKerachar	

Clan Phail

MacPhail	McFail	McFaul	Fall
Macphail	McPhaul	Fail	McPaul

Clan Davidson

Davie	Dawson	MacDade	MacDavid
Davis	Dow	Macdaid	Kay

Clan MacGillivray

Gilroy	MacGilroy	Macgilvray	Macilvrae
MacGillivoor	MacGilvra	Macilroy	

Clan Macqueen

MacCunn	MacSween	MacSwyde	Swan
MacSwan	MacSwen		

Clan MacThomas

Combe	McComb	Macombie	Thom
Combie	McCombie	Macomish	Thomas
McColm	McComie	Macthomas	Thoms
McComas	McComish	Tam	Thomson

Macleans of Dochgarroch MacIntyre, Badenoch

Note 13. Principal Shairp

John Campbell Shairp, 1819–1985, was a professor of poetry at Oxford, one of the 'Balliol Scholars', and a winner of the Newdigate Prize for Poetry in 1842. With a distinguished university career at Oxford, Edinburgh and St Andrews (he was Principal of the United College of St Andrews), this philosopher and poet gives us in this poem, of which I have quoted five verses, a deep insight into the tragedy of Culloden and its aftermath. The poem is set to music and printed in *The Songs of the North*, Vol. I, edited by A.C. Macleod and Harold Boulton, with music arranged by Malcolm Lawson.

It was Principal Shairp who asked the Rev Thomas Sinton, minister of Dores, to collect fragments of Gaelic poetry. He also thanked Cluny himself and the Rev A. Macrae of Aviemore for their help in collecting and preserving the ancient poetry, and refers gratefully to James Macpherson of Balavil for his work of conserving and popularising the Gaelic poetry of the past.

Note 14. Tartan

Tartan has been called the world's most memorable fashion. Tartan evolved from simple checks using different naturally coloured wools to more complicated 'setts' or patterns of many colours. The well known black and white check of the 'Shepherd's Plaid' is an example of the simple form, providing a clanless 'tartan' used throughout Scotland, in Highlands and Lowlands alike. Probably, as the patterns gradually became more complex, they were sterotyped to a district, and so to the people or clan living there.

Martin Martin, in his *Description of the Western Islands of Scotland* (published 1703), wrote: 'Every Isle differs from each other in their fancy of making plads, as to the stripes in breadth and colours. This humour is as different thro the main land of the Highlands, inso-far as they who have seen those places, are able, at the first view of a man's Plad to guess the place of his residence.' Even if this is an exaggeration, we can compare it to the Persian rug patterns, each peculiar to a family of a particular village.

Tartan was certainly used as a livery by chiefs from the fifteenth century onward. Identification by plant badges was perhaps cheaper and as efficient, and was also commonly used.

The Disarming Act of 1746, after the Jacobite wars, made the wearing of Tartan a penal offence. This law which was not repealed till 1785 did much to destroy the old skills and know-ledge. Weavers died, their pattern sticks would be lost, and people perhaps got out of the habit of wearing the so-identifiable Highland dress.

There was however a strong revival in the nineteenth century. George IV's visit to Scotland in 1822 saw everything festooned in Tartan; Sir Walter Scott's novels made it 'romantic', and later the Sobieski Stewarts, with somewhat unverified publications, con-ferred 'ancient' respectability. Most early designs have been given clan names retrospectively, and nowadays new Tartans are invented for all sorts of different reasons.

In an erudite and comprehensive booklet *Tartan: The Highland Habit* published by the National Museums of Scotland, Hugh Cheape writes:

'Tartan has been adopted as the national dress of all Scots, Lowland and Highland, providing a powerful form of national, cultural and personal identity. Whether traditional or a recent creation, whether a symbol of nationality or a substitute for nationhood, tartan is no mean achievement.'

Note 15. Highland Regiments and the Militia

R egular standing armies did not really exist until the seventeenth century. The history of Scots Regiments is much too long and complex to summarise, but cannot be ignored in any account of any part of the Highlands.

Following the Union of the Crowns in 1603, the first Scots regiment to be officially formed was the Royal Scots in 1625. The Scots Guards date from 1639, the Scots Greys from 1678. These were in effect Royal troops; and the Covenanting troops, the Cameronians, were a Lowland force and always anti-Jacobite.

By the late eighteenth century the population of the Highlands could not support itself on the land and young men often left to 'go for a soldier'. At first the men would probably have been the sons of those who had fought for the Stuart cause. Britain's wars increased, culminating in the Revolutionary wars against France, and the Napoleonic wars, not to mention the fighting in North America and in India. The demand for recruits grew.

1739 saw the formation of the 'Auld 42nd', the Black Watch, on the banks of the Tay. Here, in Badenoch, the Gordon Highlanders, largely raised by Jean, Duchess of Gordon, attracted many recruits. The Queen's Own Highlanders, the Seaforths, the Camerons, the Gordon Highlanders, the Argyll and Sutherland Highlanders, the Highland Light Infantry, the Glasgow Highlanders, were raised later, each by inspired leadership and on different occasions and for different reasons.

From 1739 to 1815 there were raised in the Highlands, from a population of about 380,000:

50 Battalions of the Line;
3 Battalions of Reserve;

7 Battalions of Militia;
as well as 26 battalions of Fencibles.

The 'Fencibles' were the better-trained troops whose numbers filled the gaps in the regular Army; perhaps they might be equated with the Territorial Army of today. These regiments of Fencibles were raised by the clan Chiefs who remained the patrons and the organising force behind them, each very much identifying with their own regiment.

The Militia were uniformed by their commanding officer who was re-imbursed by the government. Eliza Grant (the Highland Lady), James Boswell, and Sir Aeneas Macintosh of Macintosh, all remark on the benefits which service in the militia gave to its members, increasing their self-respect, and their standing among their peers. We may think of the Militia rather as playing the role of the Home Guard during the Second World War.

Between 1797 and 1804 there were raised for 'local defence' ten regiments including the 'Badenoch and Strathspey Volunteers – 7 Companies'. Peace with France, briefly in 1802 and then after Waterloo in 1815, led to a decline in numbers and less feeling that a volunteer force was necessary, but it revived during the Crimean War. Later Rifle Volunteer Companies were formed, of which the '6th Badenoch Company' was one. These companies found their keenest role in shooting matches.

The Highland Lady reports the drilling of the militia on the flat meadows of Dalnavert and there is emphasis on the smart appearance of the soldiery and many approving references to young men who have taken to a military career. We need to remember that the 'due of armed service' to the clan chief had been the longest lasting of the dues of service by which land was held. This service was a very important element in feudal *and* clan organisation, and lasted longer in the Highlands than anywhere else. It was abolished by the Disarming Act of 1746.

The raising of the Highland Regiments took many of the able-bodied men away from the Highlands at a time when the population was steadily out-stripping the capacity of the land to support it.

As Britain's wars multiplied in the later eighteenth and nineteenth centuries, Highland troops were a great source of strength. In 1756, the elder William Pitt, the Prime Minister, said to the House of Commons that 'from the northern mountains I have drawn a hardy and intrepid race of men, who, when left by your jealousy – became a prey to the artifices of your enemy, and had gone nigh to have over-turned the State... These men were brought to combat on your side and have served with fidelity, fought with valour and conquered for you in every part of the world.'

It may also be added that the Highland regiments restored pride to the Highlander after the appalling discrimination against him during the 'pacification' of the Highland The Regiments also encouraged the preservation and creation of pipe tunes and the general acceptance of Highland dress.

Any study of local war memorials shows the contribution of the Highlands to the fighting forces. The traditions, histories and battle honours make a tremendous statement about the Highlander and reduce me to speechless admiration, awed affection and a sense of unworthiness.

Note 16. Dr John MacKenzie

This delightful gentleman was introduced to me by Christine Byam Shaw in her book *Pigeon holes of memory: The life and times of Dr John MacKenzie, 1803–1886*, which is written from his letters and memoirs.

Dr John Mackenzie was the uncle of Osgood MacKenzie, whose book, *A Hundred Years in the Highlands* contains parts of Dr John's writings. Osgood MacKenzie wrote of his uncle that 'he was all round the most intelligent and best educated man I ever came across.'

Reading Mrs Byam Shaw's beautiful book we can learn a great deal of the 'times' of Dr John. I realise much of what he writes of the crofters and crofting methods of Gairloch, and also of Easter Ross, '*may well have been*' true of a lot of what went on here in Badenoch; but, naturally, there are many differences too, not least that of climate.

This book will greatly reward the reader.

Note 17. The Run-rig System

This is an ancient form of joint tenancy of an area, using a system of strip cultivation in which the strips, or 'rigs', were re-allocated year by year. The ground closest to the houses, usually the best arable ground, and good enough to grow oats and barley, was known as the 'in-bye', while the out-field was used as pasture. It was a pattern of land-use dating from the early Middle Ages and being a pattern created by the plough itself, was very widely used, if not universal. The 'rigs' were the raised strips of ground on which crops were grown and whose widths in time became well adapted to the use of hand-tools and hand-harvesting: the furrows acted as drains to run off the water. It was not an ideal method of farming especially as it made improvements almost impossible. As late as 1880 the Duke of Argyll could write: 'It was a system of which all the parts hung together, and which as a whole was so rooted in all the routine habits of daily and yearly life, that not one stone of it could be touched without the whole structure tumbling. Any change involved total change in the prospects and life of every family concerned.' So the improvements in farming brought with them an immense social change. Before these changes the farm cluster, or hamlet, was a rooted element of country society. The sharing made necessary by the need to spread the investment in an ox-team or a plough meant that the run-rigs were worked by the folk who lived there, and all had a share in the soil and its products. To drain, to manure, or to enclose, land was impossible to achieve while the run-rig system lasted.

Note 18. Potatoes

Potatoes were first grown in the Western Isles, and were recorded there in the early eighteenth century, certainly by 1739. They rapidly became the staple food of the poorer people. In 1840 it was estimated that potatoes formed between three-quarters and seven-eighths of the total food intake of Highland families. The cultivation of potatoes in the rigs was very easy and they were also easy to grow on lazy-beds. All travellers in the Highlands were struck by the dependence of so many on potatoes for subsistence; in 1846, the year the potato blight struck, a Badenoch minister wrote: 'Potatoes and milk may be said to constitute the principal food of the peasantry.' In Badenoch most people could only grow enough oats for about half the year, so their dependence on potatoes was even greater than in places with a better climate and soil.

In 1847 the potato crop was a total failure – the distress and disruption was appalling. Many died, while many struggled to move elsewhere. Landowners and the church attempted Poor Relief, but even when the new Poor Law was fully operating, it took some time to be effective, and there were years of terrible hardship. It must also be remembered that even when potatoes could be grown again, the short growing season here with early and late frosts, made the potato crop a chancy thing on which to base your likelihood of survival.

Note 19. Population Figures

Historically it is very difficult – if not impossible – to find satisfactory statistics, to be able to compare one area or period with another. The general impression we receive of the population of Scotland is that it is small, and of the Highlands, that it is sparse. This last statement has to be qualified; much of the land of the Highlands cannot support even subsistence farming, and the areas that can have suffered from over-population at several periods of their history.

In 1428, James I called a 'Parliament' in Inverness, on which occasion it was reckoned that there were 40–50 'leading men', each controlling about seven to eight thousand people, which would give a population of about 400,000 but it is not clear what area was being considered.

In 1630 it was estimated that the total population of the Highlands was 230,000, of which 57,000 were able-bodied men.

After the Act of Union in 1707, emigration from the Highlands southwards increased, but there is also evidence that the population in the Highlands grew, and that the Scottish population of 1,000,000 was evenly spread. By 1755 the figure is 1.3 million 'of which 33% live north of the Tay.' This changed as the industrial age developed with the rapid growth of towns, and also as the increased population in the Highlands became too great for the land to sustain. A boom in the kelp industry helped the coastal areas of the Highlands, and everywhere the increased use of potatoes helped to feed the population. Between 1787 and 1803 12,000 at least left the Highlands, and this exodus became greater after 1820. This does not take into account the terrible enforced clearances, more prevalent in the north and west than in the central Highlands. Yet the population for the Highland area continued to rise. The census for 1841 gave the population of the Highlands as 472,487, and speaks of 'congested districts' and that the population continued to rise despite the clearances and sustained emigration. Following the famine years after the potato blight of 1846, the population did fall and the alteration in land use led to many families leaving rural areas.

The development of the towns and the large concentrations of populations gave a market for beef, and the black cattle of the north were driven south to fill this need. Cattle represented capital – mobile wealth – and thus the droving trade can be called the beginning of capitalism in the Highlands and the end of the old Highland system of land use.

Here in Insh, the population figure for 1828 is given as 644, but after that the figures for the parish are combined with those of Kingussie.

The census figures for Alvie are as follows:

Population		Population	
1801	1,058	1871	882
1811	961	1881	707
1821	963	1891	656
1831	1,092	1901	533
1841	972	1911	590
1851	914	1921	670
1861	833	1931	541

In the government district of Badenoch and Strathspey the figures for 1993 are given as: Area 895 square miles.
Population: approx 11,000.

In 1993 the electoral roll covering the parish of Alvie and Insh is approx 500.

From the Statistical Account of 1835 we can learn that in Alvie:

Average births per annum	=	30
Deaths per annum	=	15
Marriages per annum	=	8

Age distribution was as follows:

Under 15	387
15–30	269
30–50	211

(+ 2 idiots). Deaths were really all due to diseases caused by poor diet.

There were 238 families; 91 employed in agriculture and 36 in trade. Sadly this leaves a great deal unexplained.

In the parish there were   13 inns
1 Justice of the Peace

1 lawyer
2 shopkeepers
2 smiths
6 weavers
4 tailors
2 brogue makers

No mason, carpenter, baker or butcher.
The lack of resident landowners was deplored.

There were   1,104 black cattle.
510 horses
7,000 sheep
101 ploughs

Note 20. Mrs Grant of Laggan: 'Letters from the Mountains'

I have quoted at length from the writings of Mrs Grant of Laggan because, while the memoirs of Eliza Grant of Rothiemurchus have been recently reprinted and are easily available, *Letters from the Mountains* has not been reprinted since 1813, and the book is difficult to find.

The portrait of Mrs Grant shown in the *Spey Valley Guide* of 1976 shows an elderly woman with a sense of humour, so that one is perhaps surprised to find that Anne Grant came to Laggan as the bride of the newly appointed minister of the parish, the Rev James Grant, in 1776, and had eight children. We read of her life as a young mother and an increasingly efficient manager of the glebe farm. She writes of her husband as 'handsomer than anybody', and often writes of his good and loving qualities, his being 'more domestic than most men', and how 'judicious and attentive' he is about all outdoor affairs, though 'totally unconcerned about affairs within', 'like a true Highlander.'

Mrs Grant writes on July 5th 1785 that 'we are building a new church'. If you visit this handsome church at Laggan Bridge as well as the small churches of this parish (and maybe the older church at Kincardine) you will realise the achievement of this modest pastor in that part of Badenoch. The building also denotes a richer, more populous district than that of Insh or even of Alvie.

Writing of a journey up the Great Glen from Fort Augustus towards Inverness in May 1773, Mrs Grant speaks of travelling 'over brown and unvaried moors for very long periods of time'. She also writes that a fellow traveller is 'astonished at my stupidity in not being lost in admiration and astonishment at the military roads'. Later in life she came to value them and admit of the great difference they made to life in the Highlands. General Caulfield, General Wade's successor, is quoted as the author of the couplet:

'If you'd seen these roads before they were made
You'd lift up your hands and bless General Wade'.

However while the road over the Corrieyairack Pass, so important to the people of Laggan, which lay at the eastern end of the parish, is one of the masterpieces of this road-building programme, it remained, to all intents and purposes, impassable in winter.

Inverness is described as being 'most agreeably situated at the very threshold of this rugged territory...', but 'exposed to such chilling blasts, as made us reflect with pleasure on the shelter we receive from our mountains'. It is 'somehow a cheerful looking place, because the people look cheerful; yet not flourishing, though no situation can be better adapted for the purpose of commerce.' The society is 'genteel and one meets many well-bred agreeable people.' Oban, she writes, has 'now become a large and flourishing village; it is the capital of Lorne in Argyllshire.' It is interesting to read of Cawdor Castle as 'a venerable and gloomy edifice of grey renown' and her fancy that 'demons of black despairing melancholy dwell in some of those caverns that echo to the roar of Calder water.' Castle Grant is 'a spacious, convenient, and elegant mansion... where everything evinces an abode, where baronial pomp and hospitality still continue to linger, softened by the milder graces of modern elegance.' (August 1785)

Mrs Grant's comments reveal the nature of life in the Highlands at the end of the eighteenth century. There are no references to the Jacobite troubles of the '45 and after; there are a few references to the emergence of the United States of America; there are several references to the Napoleonic Wars... 'this fatal war...' showing that even in the centre of Scotland this epic struggle had its effect.

Of the Highland character this observant and thoughtful lady writes 'The Highlanders resemble the French in being poor with better grace than others.' She writes admiringly of Highland pride in ancestry and of the songs which enshrine this in legend and tradition among the present generation. She endeavours to have her eldest son brought up to speak Gaelic, and is distressed when he returns from a Glasgow visit 'speaking only English'. She makes the comment (more than once) that hardship, hunger and persecution develop the spirit and give rise to a sense of poetry. The Highlanders seem to her to be a race of poets – song and story are in their lifeblood. Mrs Grant writes with sympathy and understanding of many songs of all types, and of the habit of singing to accompany any task. The song 'Crodh Challein' – 'Colin's Cattle' – was the lullaby to which one of Mrs Grant's sons died, and ever after it moved her to tears; it can still have that effect on many today.

Dr Johnson noted, as she did, the ease with which people of all ranks mixed. Dr I.F. Grant, in *Periods in Highland History*, notes that 'The distinguished manners of the people are mentioned by nearly every early visitor'.

The relative duties and roles of men and women in the rural society around her intrigued Anne Grant; 'a Highlander never sits at a loom; it would be like putting a deer in the plough.' 'Fighting, hunting, lounging in the sun, music and poetry make up a man's life. Woman's province is thus extended – both in actual labour and in management.' 'The custom of leaving everything to the more helpless sex continues...'

Highlanders talk of 'countries', not of parish communities; language and manners differ greatly between particular clans; the pattern was of a general dislike of the *neighbouring* clans, and some better relationships with the ones beyond. There are several notable comments revealing Mrs Grant's affection for and admiration of the people she lived among.

'Ties of blood are stronger and duties and relationships better understood in the Highlands than anywhere else.' 'The lower class of Highlanders excels all others.'

November 19th 1791: 'The only cause of complaint in Scotland is the rage for sheep farming... the plight of the evicted is made worse in that poor people have not the language, money, nor education to push their way anywhere else.' 'The Highlanders possess feelings and principles that might almost rescue human nature from the reproach which false philosophy and false refinement have brought upon it.'

Finally, two general comments appealed to me and reveal the set of mind of this admirable lady ; 'Amiable men are very scarce indeed', her husband being one. And 'Modern minds will not be long enough quiet to allow the cream to rise.'

Note 21. Principal Baird

Principal Baird, of whom Dr John Macdonald, Minister of Alvie, wrote in 1835 in the second Statistical Survey, was a brilliant scholar who entered Edinburgh University (via Bo'ness village school and Linlithgow Grammar School) in 1775. In 1786 he was licensed by the parish of Linlithgow and in 1787 ordained to the parish of Dunkeld. Later he was transferred to the New Greyfriars Church in Edinburgh, and later again to the High Church. In 1877 he was also elected Professor of Oriental Languages at Edinburgh University and in 1793, at the age of 33, he was appointed Principal of the University. He became Moderator of the General Assembly of the Church of Scotland in 1800.

His later years were principally occupied 'in promoting the extension of religious education among the poorer classes of his fellow-country men in the Highlands and Islands'. In May 1824 he presented a scheme to the General Assembly affirming that 'he had found nearly a hundred thousand human beings unable to read or write, and innumerable districts where the people could not hear a sermon above once a year, and had seen thousands of habitations where a Sabbath bell was never heard.' In 1832 the thanks of the General Assembly were conveyed to him by Dr Chalmers, the moderator: 'The benefits you have conferred on the cause of education in the Highlands and Islands of Scotland will forever associate your name with the whole of that immense region, and hand down your memory to distant ages as the moral benefactor of many thousand families.'

'By his benevolent exertions the worthy principal is said to have contributed much to the freeing of the minds of the Highlanders from the superstitions they were so fond of cherishing, and particularly to the expulsion of the fairies from the Highland hills.'

It is recorded that Principal Baird himself visited, in 1827, the Highlands of Argyllshire, the western parts of Inverness and Ross, and the Western Isles, from Lewis to Kintyre. In 1828, he visited the north Highlands and Orkney and Shetland. It is thus probable that he himself never crossed Drumochter or travelled through Badenoch, though as the founder and first Convenor of the General Assembly's Highlands and Islands Committee his work and encouragement would have been felt here.

Note 22. Ossian

James Macpherson was born in 1736 in Badenoch. For a short time, as a young man, he was a teacher at Ruthven, and later a tutor to the Graham family of Balnagowan. About 1756 he showed a friend what he said was a translation he had made of a ballad on the death of Oscar, a character of the great 'Fenian Cycle', the collection of oral poetry, song and story about the circle and exploits of Fionn MacCoul (who is the Fingal of James

Macpherson's epic poems).

The translations published in 1760 of 'Fragments of Ancient Poetry collected in the Highlands of Scotland, translated from the Gaelic or Erse language' purported to be compositions of epic poetry by the third-century bard Ossian. They won great acclaim and excited much interest. James Macpherson said he knew of more and longer poems, and he was encouraged (partly by gifts of money) to travel the Highlands to research and collect these.

In 1762 and 1763 he published *Fingal*, an epic in six parts, and *Temora*. The vogue for these books was enormous. They were translated into Italian in 1763, into French in 1777; and later into Czech in 1827, into Hungarian in 1833, and Polish in 1844. It is recorded that Napoleon's favourite bedtime reading was the Italian version of 'Fingal'. The islands we now refer to as the Falklands were for a while given the name of the Ossianic heroine, Malvina.

Mrs Grant of Laggan and the friends of her unmarried days were much enamoured of characters of Macpherson's epics, and they are frequently referred to in her letters. Later, when she was living at Laggan, she was proud to know Sir James Macpherson and writes of her admiration of the man as well as of his writings.

Though critics contrast the style and shape of Macpherson's poems with the ancient poetic forms (he never published the originals), the effect was to develop an enthusiasm for the Gaelic language and for Highland culture generally, not only in song and story. It actually did result in the preservation of ancient collections of Gaelic manuscripts and oral fragments, as well as a revival of interest and understanding of Gaelic literature of many kinds, of music and of the patterns of clan and family living.

It must be remembered that the eighteenth century was a time when Shakespeare was also re-written 'to suit modern audiences', and the embellishment by many authors of earlier literary treasures was quite commonplace and not thought to be wrong in any way.

Certainly James Macpherson 'did well' out of his writing, true translations or no. He became an MP for Camelford, a landowner in Badenoch, and was buried in Westminster Abbey in 1796.

Note 23. Employment

The twentieth century has shown tremendous changes in the types of employment available in this district. The estates of Rothiemurchus, Kinrara, Alvie, Dunachton and Balavil carry records showing the numbers employed by the estate at various times, and usually the type of work done.

There are some very striking changes between c1950 and 1994. No full-time gardeners, but secretaries and accountants. No carters or coachmen, but tractor-drivers and motor maintenance men. Land, forest and computer consultants, and computer programmers make their appearance. There is usually one game-keeper instead of three. Farm workers are down from about 9 or 10 to 2 or 3. One saw-miller remains but the estate carpenters and saw-mill assistants who would probably have lived on the estates seem to have vanished. Shepherds manage more sheep than before. Transport is the key to most of these changes.

The management (and cleaning) of holiday cottages, let for short periods, is now part of a major industry hereabouts. The running of the caravan park at Dalraddy is part of the diversification recommended for the use of land. The Kincraig Stores is also a 'Tourist Information Centre', a recent development. Part-time work everywhere is giving people the extra income needed, whether it be on the farm, in forestry, domestic work, secretarial or gardening. People from this parish work in Kingussie, Newtonmore, Aviemore, and further afield – Inverness, Grantown-on-Spey and Pitlochry, and some from those areas come to work here; again improved transport makes all this possible.

Unemployment is not high by national standards, but there is a constant stream of incomers looking for work. Young people leaving school can for the most part find work, but if further training or tertiary education is required, the young must leave the district; usually this means that they will live and work later elsewhere – this drift away is still a large factor in employment here.

There is also a change in 'house-work'. The 'Big House' which was only occupied by the family for part of the year, was staffed in the season by a team brought from the south. Headed by a butler and a housekeeper, it consisted of two or three footmen, a lady's maid, housemaids of various rankings, a cook and several kitchen staff. This team has been replaced by the owner's wife with two or three part-time workers, plus extra help on special occasions. The 'Big House' has to be used to provide income instead of 'leisure pleasure' for the family.

This is true of the sporting rights of an estate also.

Note 24. The Snowstorm of 1976

A very heavy snow-fall, on top of an existing cover of snow, on Saturday night and Sunday March 5th/6th cut Badenoch off from the outside world. It blocked all roads, and the railways too. It meant that the hundreds (perhaps thousands) of skiers in Aviemore and elsewhere who had planned to leave on Sunday night could not do so. It was Wednesday or Thursday before anybody could move out.

The hotels in Aviemore ran out of food before Monday morning and bought up all reserves of food in the Aviemore shops which they could reach. Guesthouses seemed to have been carrying slightly more stocks, but no supplies were available from outside.

However it was later realised that most ordinary households were sufficiently 'old-fashioned' to carry plentiful supplies and were quite unfazed by the stopping of outside supplies. They also carried candles and alternative methods of heating. (Power-cuts lasted from four to eight days, in places more.) This self-sufficiency in country-dwellers may well be one of the things to change in the future (the influence and importance of transport again!) However, managing without daily visits to foodstores is part of the way of life that does attract people to come to live here.

Note 25. Book List

The many gaps I have left will be well filled by reading the following most valuable and fascinating books, which are listed in no special order.

Letters from the Mountains, Mrs Anne Grant of Laggan. (1813)
Difficult to obtain. Late-eighteenth-century letters with vivid comments on many sides of contemporary society; written from the parish of Laggan.

Memoirs of a Highland Lady, (Vols. I and II), Elizabeth Grant of Rothiemurchus. (1988 edition. Cannongate classics)
Wonderful, lively and thoughtful account of the Rothiemurchus estate and the changing society in which the author lived, 1797–1830.

Queen Victoria's Highland Journals, ed. David Duff. (Michael Joseph, 1994, Lomond Books)
A vivid account of the countryside and people by a shrewd observer who so much enjoyed this area.

In the Glens where I was young, Meta Scarlett. (Siskin, 1988)
A marvellous collection of history, legends, folklore, traditions and anecdote by someone who really belongs to the glens hereabouts; all concisely gathered in a small volume of outstanding value. Much recommended.

Laggan – Past and Present, Dr Ian Richardson.
Compiled and written for the Laggan Community Association, 1990
An excellent detailed and vivid description of the parish of Laggan, past and present.

Candie for the Foundling, Anne Gordon. (Pentland Press, 1992)
An immensely detailed and fascinating survey of the whole work

of the ministers and Kirk Sessions throughout Scotland, from the beginning of the Church of Scotland to the present day.

Pigeonholes of Memory. The Life and Times of Dr John MacKenzie 1803–1886, Christine Byam Shaw
Not concerned with this area but so lively and illuminating an account of this period that we gain increased understanding of the Highlands in his times.

Burt's Letters from the North of Scotland. (Vols I and II) First published in 1754. Reprinted 1974. (John Donald Publishers Ltd., Edinburgh)
First-hand information on the appearance of people and places as seen by the traveller. An accurate and important source of information.

Antiquities and Scenery of the North of Scotland, in a series of Letters to Thomas Pennant, Esq, by the Rev Chas. Cordiner, Minister of St Andrew's Chapel, Banff. (1780)
Though this covers a great deal of Scotland without reaching Badenoch at all, there is a great deal to be learnt of the conditions of life and the inter-linking of communities.

Drove Roads of Scotland, A.B. Haldane. (Nelson, 1952)
New Ways through the Glens, A.B. Haldane. (Nelson, 1952)
Classics, both of them; the chapters on this area are splendid.

Highways and Byways of Scotland, Seton Gordon
Another classic, guaranteed to make you want to walk; the legends told may differ from other versions, but that is how it should be.

The Cairngorms: Their natural history and scenery, Desmond Nethersole-Thompson & Adam Watson. (Collins, 1974)
A brilliant authoritative and comprehensive account of this great area.

Highland Folkways, I.F. Grant. (Routledge and Keegan Paul Ltd., 1975)
This is a detailed and scholarly study yielding great pleasure as well as a clearer understanding of so many details of everyday life; a most fascinating book.

Everyday life on an old Highland Farm 1769–1782, I.F. Grant. (1924 Longmans Green. New edition 1974)
A brilliantly researched book giving life to the work on the Dunachton estate from the account books of the farm, and placing it in the context of that time of radical change.

Tartan. The Highland Habit, Hugh Cheape. (National Museums of Scotland, 1991)
This fresh interpretation of the world's most memorable fabric tells a story that is fascinating, colourful and distinctively Scottish.

Periods in Highland History, I.F.Grant and Hugh Cheape. (Shepheard-Walwyn, 1987)
Scholarly and very well-written insights into the history of the Highlands. Eminently readable, we are led through seven periods of history, with much fascinating detail, much of it relating specifically to this area.

The Kingdom of the Picts, Anna Ritchie. (Chambers, The Way It Was Series)
A primary school book which gives most clearly the basic facts as well as the historical spirit of the Picts. Brilliant work with wonderful illustrations.

Beyond the Highland Line, Caroline Bingham. (Constable)
An excellent book; much recommended.

Glimpses of Church and Social Life in the Highlands in olden times, Alexander Macpherson. (1893)
Difficult to obtain; very valuable to study.

In the shadow of Cairngorm, W. Forsyth. (1900)
A detailed account of the parish of Abernethy and Kincardine, with many references to the surrounding areas.

The Poetry of Badenoch, Rev Thomas Sinton.
A large collection, Gaelic, with Sinton's translations.

Scotland through the Ages, Michael Jenner. (A Mermaid Book, Michael Joseph Ltd)
A beautifully and prolifically illustrated history of Scotland, giving a very good overall view. You should note that there are few references to this area. A delightful book to possess.

The New History of Scotland. General Editor Jenny Wormald
Advisory Editors G.W.S. Barrow, Christopher Smout.(Edward Arnold, 1984)
1. Warlords and Holy Men. Scotland 80–1000. Alfred P. Smyth
2. Kingship and Unity. Scotland 1000–1306. G.W.S. Barrow
3. Independence and Nationhood. Scotland 1306–1469. Alexander Grant
4. Court, Kirk, and Community. Scotland, 1470–1625. Jenny Wormald
5. Lordship to Patronage. Scotland 1603–1745. Rosalind Mitchison
6. Integration, Enlightenment and Industrialization. Scotland 1746–1832. Bruce Lenman
7. Industry and Ethos. Scotland 1832–1914. Sydney and Olive Checkland
8. No Gods and Precious Few Heroes. Scotland 1914–1980. C. Harvie

Easily obtainable and up-to-date general histories of Scotland.

Also appropriate volumes of the publications of the Inverness Field Club; the Scottish Historical Review and of the Scottish Gaelic Society. Proceedings of Society Antiquaries of Scotland.
All these books, especially the volumes of the New History of

Scotland carry extensive lists for further reading and study.

There is also an old novel, *The New Road* by Neil Munro, which gives a vivid insight into what happened in the Highlands with the coming of the new roads of the eighteenth century. Blackwood. 1914.

ACKNOWLEDGEMENTS

This is not an academic book so there are no footnotes showing the sources of all the information gathered.

I would acknowledge most gratefully the most notable books of Dr I.F. Grant and Dr Hugh Cheape who have given life to so much knowledge of this area; they are frequently referred to in the text and have been a constant source of inspiration as well as information. I am very grateful to Dr Cheape for his advice and encouragement.

The account of Montrose's campaigns is largely based on John Buchan's biography (published by Nelson) – I acknowledge my indebtedness.

The maps are drawn by Wendy Price for whose help and understanding I am most grateful.

I must thank David Hayes for his generous support and encouragement and the use of his photographs, of which I have long been an admirer.

I am very grateful to many people in the parish for their help in supplying local details, especially concerning nineteenth- and twentieth-century matters.

I must also thank the staff of the National Library of Scotland and at the Inverness Library, and Mrs Ann Wakeling at the Aviemore Library. Thanks are also due to Mr Ross Noble of the Highland Folk Museum at Kingussie for his support and advice.

I would also gratefully acknowledge the support and contribution of the Highland Regional Council.

INDEX